Moving from What to What If?

This practical book outlines how you can challenge students to grapple with complex problems and engage more meaningfully with information across the content areas, rather than rely solely on rote memorization and standardized testing to measure academic success. Author John Barell shares vignettes from effective middle and high school teachers around the country, analyzes what works and what doesn't when encouraging students to dig deeper, and offers practical strategies that you can try in your own classroom.

Topics include:

♦ Guiding students to hone their skills in abstract reasoning, inquiry, creative problem solving, and critical thinking;

♦ Designing your lessons and units for authentic achievement, to prepare students for success in their future careers and academic pursuits;

♦ Using rigorous benchmark assessments to analyze students' progress in meaningful ways; and

♦ Encouraging students to set learning goals and drive their own achievement.

Aligned with the Common Core and other standards, this book will help you teach students to become inquisitive, engaged citizens who wonder about the universe, stretch their imaginations, and solve problems by asking, *What If?*

John Barell is Professor Emeritus of Curriculum and Teaching at Montclair State University, and a former public school teacher in New York City.

Other Eye On Education Books
Available from Routledge
(www.routledge.com/eyeoneducation)

Moving from What to *What If?*

Teaching Critical Thinking
with Authentic Inquiry
and Assessments

John Barell

 Routledge
Taylor & Francis Group

NEW YORK AND LONDON

First published 2016
by Routledge
711 Third Avenue, New York, NY 10017

and by Routledge
2 Park Square, Milton Park, Abingdon, Oxon, OX14 4RN

Routledge is an imprint of the Taylor & Francis Group, an informa business

Library of Congress Cataloging-in-Publication Data
Names: Barell, John, author.
Title: Moving from what to what if : teaching critical thinking
    with authentic inquiry and assessments / by John Barell.
Description: New York, NY : Routledge, 2016. | Includes bibliographical references.
Identifiers: LCCN 2015034202| ISBN 9781138998605 (hardback) |
    ISBN 9781138998612 (pbk.) | ISBN 9781315658612 (e-book)
Subjects: LCSH: Critical thinking—Study and teaching. | Learning, Psychology of.
Classification: LCC LB1590.3 .B364 2016 | DDC 370.15/2—dc23
LC record available at http://lccn.loc.gov/2015034202

ISBN: 978-1-138-99860-5 (hbk)
ISBN: 978-1-138-99861-2 (pbk)
ISBN: 978-1-315-65861-2 (ebk)

Typeset in Palatino LT Std
by Apex CoVantage, LLC

Printed and bound in the United States of America by Publishers Graphics,
LLC on sustainably sourced paper.

Dedication

For my secondary school teachers who taught me to reason critically:
Ray Chapman
Claire Slattery Heffernan
Wilbury A. Crockett

And to Albert Einstein whose thought experiments—
"What if?"—changed my entire way of thinking.

Epigraph

Education is a wonderfully unpredictable act. One never knows the answer he will receive to a question. This is in many ways the beauty of education. When we look at the act of educating as one in which we (teachers and students) ask questions, both about a certain subject matter and the world around us, we can never know where these questions will lead. It is through this questioning, through education, that we welcome students into the world that we share, and hand over to them the responsibility and awesome power to begin something new—to create, question, answer, write, speak, analyze, think, and be critical in ways that can never be predicted.

Stephen Lazar
Teacher, Social Studies
New York City
2015
Inspired by political theorist Hannah Arendt

Contents

eResources

A student interpretation tool and sample response are available on our website as free eResources. You can access the eResources by visiting the book product page on our website: www.routledge.com/products/9781138998612. Click on the tab that says "eResources" and select the files. They will begin downloading to your computer.

Meet the Author

John Barell is an international consultant to schools interested in teaching inquiry, critical thought and reflection.

A native New Yorker, Barell has sailed to Antarctica as part of Operation Deepfreeze to explore that continent based upon his meetings and correspondences with Rear Admiral Richard E. Byrd. After Antarctica, he became an educator in New York City public high schools, then at Montclair State University in teacher education and world literature (now Professor Emeritus). Subsequently (2000–2007), he was a consultant at the American Museum of Natural History where he fostered networks of inquiry among science and social studies educators.

Currently, he is researching the various ways we assess the quality and improvement of students' performances with 21st-century skills: inquiry, problem solving, critical/creative thought and technological proficiency. The first completed report on this project, *How Do We Know They're Getting Better? Assessment for 21st century minds, K–8* (Corwin), was published January, 2012.

This volume, *Moving from* What *to* What If?*: Teaching Critical Thinking with Authentic Inquiry and Assessment*, is the final report of this study.

Sailing to Antarctica has served as his model for inquiry: starting with a dream and a passion leading to explorations of new territories—physical, spiritual, educational and creative.

Barell is author of these publications about Antarctica: *Quest for Antarctica—A Journey of Wonder and Discovery* (memoir, 2011, ebook); *Surviving Erebus—An Antarctic Adventure on board HMS Erebus and Terror* (YA novel, 2008, 2012, ebook) and "Twenty Below," an award-winning story published by *Boys' Life* and *Boys' Life Anthology*.

He is also the author of these professional books: *Why Are School Buses Always Yellow? Teaching for inquiry, K–8* (2016, 2nd edn); *Did You Ever Wonder? Fostering curiosity here, there and everywhere* (2013); *How Do We Know They're Getting Better? Assessment for 21st century minds, K–8* (2012); *Problem-Based Learning—An inquiry approach* (2007); *Developing More Curious Minds* (2003);

"... EVER WONDER...?" (1992); *Opening the American Mind* (1988) and *Playgrounds of Our Minds* (1980).

A recent (2013) novel, *Absolute Bearing,* is available at Amazon.com.

John Barell
Lt. USN-(Ret.)

jbarell@nyc.rr.com
www.morecuriousminds.com
http://morecuriousminds.blogspot.com
http://antarcticdreams.com
www.absolutebearing.info
@johnbarell

Preface

This journey began after completing what I would consider the first leg of the adventure, a study of how we can learn about students' growth over time using a wide variety of assessment experiences: *How Do We Know They're Getting Better? Assessment for 21st century minds, K–8* (2012).

The next logical step toward understanding was to graduate to secondary school and ask, "How do we know older students are getting better at these 21st-century intellectual abilities, ones like inquiry, problem solving, critical reasoning, imaginative thinking, and reflection?"

I began seeking out those models of excellence who could help tell the story of how they engage their students with rigorous intellectual work and use authentic assessments, ones that challenge students to think productively about complex problems and issues and not merely check off an answer in a multiple choice bubble test.

It was not difficult to identify many teachers who challenge their students to think productively and believe in the overall goal of assessing students' growth, but not by relying on standardized tests. I was always so delighted when these educators spoke up, because they are evidence that those who speak so generally about our schools—"They're failing"—are incorrect and only attempting to create bumper-sticker headlines for their own gain.

Along the way, many felt the challenge and use of their time were too taxing. But we were blessed with the outstanding educators who stayed the course and whose stories you will read herein.

These are men and women who have moved away from the lower levels of intellectual challenge (see Bloom, Three Story Intellect) toward "the ability to test hypotheses, analyze and synthesize in order to be successful not just on the new assessments, but also in college and in future careers" (Marzano & Toth, 2014).

These are educational leaders who exemplify the best of what Newmann and his associates (1996) called "authentic achievement," that is, thinking hard and long about complex issues demanding problem solving and critical reasoning, not merely memorization of stuff.

In the chapter on professional development (Thirteen), you will meet a German foreign exchange student visiting in Pike County Schools, GA. Her assessment of the differences between the rigor demanded of her back home and what she encountered here in her host school (mostly "multiple choice") is eye-opening and drove the Superintendent of Schools, Dr. Michael Duncan, to initiate massive district-wide change toward "authentic intellectual work."

Those I've Met

In no particular order here are brief descriptions of those who have taken the challenge to craft their own means of determining how well students have grown intellectually and emotionally:

Tim, a government teacher, who sends his students out into the Sandusky, OH, community regularly to identify needs and work to meet them—to reduce the number of concussions on the football field, for example, or to prevent automobile accidents at dangerous intersections.

Hannah, a language arts teacher, who challenged her students to Tweet scenes from *Macbeth*, act them out and apply major themes to their own lives.

Mike, a teacher of Physics 1 and 2, whose students learn how to analyze physical forces exemplified in the swinging pendulum and apply this inquiry process to a wider variety of phenomena.

Andy, whose students analyze complex issues like the federal government's providing food stamps, stated claims and counter claims presenting good reasons and reliable evidence for same, the essence of critical thinking.

Laura, whose idea of a high level pre assessment is to ask students to create their own ideal communities, with schools, hospitals, fire and police facilities and to explain their reasoning in mathematical terms.

Josh, a teacher who provides students with opportunities to hypothesize and set up their own experiments (determine the effects of various spices on bacteria, for example) and at the same time learn how to frame results as claims and counter claims.

Hannah and Sue, who have developed a fine-tuned system for enhancing students' abilities to set goals for the improvement of their own academic performance.

Steve, who recently (2015) testified before the US Senate sub-committee on education about the re-authorization of No Child Left Behind, and taught history backwards, commencing with an intriguing episode in Crimea that led students to guide their learning with their own questions.

Katy, a physics teacher, whose students regularly apply their learnings to the district elementary school playgrounds to make improvements.

Beth, a language arts teacher whose benchmark assessments regularly asked students to critique literary texts in accordance with the CCSS criterion: "Cite strong and thorough textual evidence to support analysis of what the text says explicitly as well as inferences drawn from the text."

Lanett, an International Baccalaureate biology teacher, who presented her students with opportunities to design experiments within a desert biome or habitat.

David, a social studies teacher, who engaged his students in the authenticity of conducting role plays and mock trials on historic figures like Cortez, Martin Luther and a former Nazi party sympathizer.

Michael, a school superintendent, who, upon learning that school work for students was "boring . . . busy work," undertook massive programmatic change toward "authentic intellectual work."

Hannah and Madie, two high school students who worked at the leading edge of knowledge creation with astrophysicists from Arizona State University, Harvard and Cal Tech to identify new stars in the cosmos. Such research "greatly enhanced our skills such as thinking scientifically, accepting failure, resourcefulness, organization, collaborative skills, time management, communication skills and many others."

Of special note here are Hannah and Madie's comments on how we learn: by making mistakes, learning from them and pressing forward.

And, in the Final Words, Francesca, a graduate of one of the studied schools, who tells us of how she became a "deep and open thinker" as the result of working on authentic problems with peers and of very high expectations from her mentors.

These are educators and students who can tell us how to challenge students to engage the "cognitive complexity" demanded in today's world. They all can answer the question put by some teachers frustrated with the higher levels of intellectual work demanded by Common Core State Standards:

> Where is the "HOW?" Many of my fellow teachers and I understand the need for more rigor and challenging our students to help them achieve. We get it. What is lacking is the "how." How is teaching with the new standards different from teaching with the old? (Marzano & Toth, 2014, p. 9)

This book is not an exact translation of new standards into the classroom, but each of the aforementioned teachers could always tell me exactly which standards applied: CCSS, Next Generation Science Standards or C3 College, Career and Civic Life Framework for Social Studies State Standards.

What We've Learned

Perhaps the most significant learning to emerge from these three years of research is that all teachers have the opportunity to engage their students in productive thinking about complex problems and issues. They also possess the means of assessing their students' growth using their own non-standardized, informal yet very direct evaluations. When Steve testified before the Senate committee he called these assessments "rigorous" and "college level." They are not the multiple choice kinds of "bubble tests" our guest from Germany observed during her stay in the United States.

We learned that each subject challenges us to ask similar kinds of questions in order to acquire new knowledge and understanding: in the sciences and humanities we must ask, "How do we know?" What evidence do we have to support our claims, counter claims, conclusions, causal connections, and future predictions?

This is the question a young high school student, Elizabeth Ferguson, my mother, asked her scientist father (inventor of D-Zerta) when he claimed that each snow flake falling outside their house in LeRoy, NY "was unique."

"How do you know?" she asked directly. "Have you seen them all?" No, of course not. She asked me the very same questions when I told her on a tour of the American Museum of Natural History here in New York, that each grain of sand on any beach was "unique."

"How do you know? Have you seen them all?"

So, in every walk of life it's important to ask what my mother and each of our excellent models of teaching for authenticity have done, to challenge students to think rigorously, to question the unknown as well as that which we take for granted, the disparities and contradictions in our daily lives.

Questioning—inquiry—is very much a part of what each teacher does, not only posing her own, but challenging students to do the same.

As Steve reflected,

education is a wonderfully unpredictable act. One never knows the answer he will receive to a question. This is in many ways the beauty of education. When we look at the act of educating as one in which we [teachers and students] ask questions, both about a certain subject matter and the world around us, we can never know where these questions will lead. It is through this questioning, through education, that we welcome students into the world that we share, and hand over to them the responsibility and awesome power to begin something new—to create, question, answer, write, speak, analyze, think, and be critical in ways that can never be predicted. (Personal communication, June, 2015)

I welcome you to partake of this journey and urge you as teachers and supervisors of various subjects to pay particular attention not only to areas of your own expertise, but to those areas you have not taught.

Why? Because one of my themes for the past three years conducting this research has been to search for and find the common elements amongst all subjects we teach:

♦ The major intellectual processes: inquiry, problem solving, critical/creative/reflective thought.

♦ A focus upon student-led inquiry.

♦ Modeling good instruction in whatever subject.

♦ Enhancing cognitive development, developing what we call proportional reasoning, a capability evident during adolescence, Piaget's stage of Formal Operations.

♦ Intense commitment to what Fred Newmann and his associates (1996) called "authentic achievement," the work of adults in the world of work: problem solving, thinking critically, being creative.

♦ Use of rigorous benchmark assessments for pre formative and summary assessments.

These are the threads woven throughout each story and described in greater detail in Chapters Three through Five of this volume.

I hope you will join me in an adventure, one clearly demonstrating the highest caliber of educator in this country, from student to teacher to administrative leader, from the suburbs to the inner city, including the vast diversity of students we all educate.

Welcome and be enriched.

John Barell
Southampton, NY
August, 2015

References

Marzano, R. and Toth, M.D. (2014) "Teaching for Rigor: A call for a critical instructional shift." West Palm Beach, FL: The Marzano Center. www.marzanocenter.com/files/Teaching-for-Rigor-20140318.pdf (accessed October, 2015).

Newmann, F. and associates (1996) *Authentic Achievement—Restructuring schools for intellectual quality*. San Francisco, CA: Jossey-Bass.

Chapter 1

Teachers as Argonauts of Change

At the end of her social studies project involving bringing about change in her local community of Sandusky, OH, a student named Sabrina reflected on what it meant to convince civic leaders to do more to avoid traffic accidents:

> At the end of the project, *I learned that any citizen can make a change.* This project has helped me realize that even students can improve a problem in a community, which was unexpected. I honestly never knew that students could make a change until the panel told my group that we should keep pushing this intersection problem to make it more successful. The panel has motivated me to make a change. (emphasis added)

How did her teacher, Tim Obergefell, help guide Sabrina and her classmates, working in teams on different civic problems, to reflect in this way on her role as a citizen?

What kinds of authentic learning experiences, focusing upon which 21st-century skills and dispositions, had he fostered within his class in order help Sabrina successfully navigate the complexities of social change within her community?

And how had working collaboratively with her classmates helped Sabrina achieve this much-desired sense of efficacy (agency), a disposition toward realizing you are in control of your own destiny and, with others, can be instrumental in effecting change for the good?

After this experience, Sabrina is light years removed from being the passive adolescent who slumps back in her chair feeling, "I'm not good at much. Life is what it is."

Tim, his colleagues, her parents and classmates have helped Sabrina achieve a momentous goal of education—realizing you can make a difference, that you are in command of your own life, you write your own story.

This book is an attempt to understand how Tim and the other educators are helping their students achieve similar goals, to think through some of life's most complex problems and issues and not merely come to class having memorized all the functions of local, state and federal government expecting to spout them back on Friday's test.

That Which Unites Us

Having been an English teacher for several years, a teacher educator for over a quarter century, and subsequently a consultant to the American Museum of Natural History here in New York City I find myself in a fascinating position as an educator, that of seeking out commonalities amidst all life experiences.

I'm not sure if this passion for that which transcends strict subject matter boundaries arises from my own teaching, from being a generalist as a teacher educator or from some other source. In this role you tend to seek out what unites all of our educational endeavors, not what separates us into different, distinct categories. How is the biology teacher like the language, arts and math teachers?

Maybe it has to do with having grown up with another passion—that for Antarctic exploration—at a very early age, a driving inquiry that led me to meet America's foremost polar explorer, Admiral Richard E. Byrd, and to sail south on his flagship, *USS Glacier*, during Operation Deep-Freeze.[1] It might have been this very early drive to ask hundreds of questions of scientists, sailors, historians and authors about the life in and history of Antarctica that led me toward being a person who is fascinated with different points of view, different perspectives on this captivating, mysterious land.

Or, it might be from engaging in the kind of research Hannah and Madie did on discovering new stars that we realize how interdisciplinary our problems are—they demand language, math, historical and scientific analysis.

So, whatever the source, I find myself wondering about that which unites us, as educators, as human beings in the search for meaning and understanding.

21st Century or World Class Skills and Capacities

Thus, this is a book that focuses upon the intellectual processes that we all engage in, in all walks of life as well as in education.

Socrates supposedly said, "The unexamined life is not worth living." This means that one way of enhancing the meaningfulness of life is continually to reflect on what we have done and plan to do.

In the accounts written down by Plato, Socrates educated young people of Athens about the good life, appropriate ways of thinking and governing ourselves. In all his dialogues we can today read how he is challenging all of us to pose those questions that need to be considered to lead productive lives.

"I infect people," Socrates said, "with the same perplexities I experience" (Arendt, 1977, p. 179).

Hannah Arendt noted that Socrates' commitment to opening the eyes of Athenian youth was, in fact, "the only way thinking can be taught" (ibid.), to share with them the fascinating mysteries and questions about living the good life.

Thus, today we are still learning how to challenge students to inquire, think critically, imaginatively, pose and resolve problems and reflect on these experiences. These are, indeed, "world class" skills.

We speak today of "21st century skills or capacities," but to my mind our focus on inquiry, problem posing/resolving and critical/creative/reflective thought all emanate from Socrates and those whose recorded thoughts we have from so long ago. "How large is the earth?" asked Eratosthenes. Through ingenious problem solving he figured it out without a calculator, nor a computer, and was pretty close to accurate, some say within 1.6% (www.windows2universe.org/citizen_science/myw/w2u_eratosthenes_calc_earth_size.html, accessed June, 2015).

So, what's changed? Well, today we have within our hands on a smart phone more computing power than NASA was able to load onto Apollo 11 on its mission to the moon in 1969.

That's why 21st century skills are so important, because we have access to virtually unlimited amounts of information in seconds.

But what do we do with it?

Think about it productively as Socrates has taught us.

Participant School Mission Statements

Another reason for focusing so intently upon said skills is that we find them within most schools' statements of their missions:

> Students in all grades apply inquiry and learn to use information–communication technologies safely and effectively.
>
> Our mission is equipping every student with the knowledge, skills, and character essential to being a responsible citizen of our community, our nation, and the world.

Incorporate 21st century competences, including self-assessment, goal setting, conferencing and collaboration into teaching and learning and develop tools to provide consistent and meaningful feedback in these areas.

Therefore, it has always made sense to this author to ask and answer the question, "How do we know they're getting better?" about these various skills, now called "21st century capacities."

We note again that the cognitive skills herein identified—inquiry, problem solving, critical/creative/reflective thought—are the same as in ancient Greece when Socrates held forth in Athens.

Living as Responsible Citizens

Being a "responsible citizen" calls for students to be proficient not only in reciting and then explaining the historical/cultural/philosophical roots of our Declaration of Independence (or Constitution), but also being able to analyze these for their strengths, flaws and ways of improvement. More significantly, perhaps, is the requirement to be able to analyze all data drawn from many websites, authors and so-called experts. Are they accurate, biased, representative?

This approach was brilliantly summarized in the Greenwich, CT, "Vision of a Graduate" wherein this district asserts that in addition to knowing stuff, possessing declarative knowledge, and, I assume, attaining deep understanding about content concepts, we want students to be able to:

Pose and pursue substantive questions

Critically interpret, evaluate, and synthesize information

Explore, define, and solve complex problems

Generate innovative, creative ideas and products

Communicate and collaborate with others

Conduct selves in ethical, responsible manner

Respect other cultures and points of view

Pursue unique interests, passions and curiosities . . .

(2006, adapted from: www.greenwichschools.org/
page.cfm?p=8937, accessed December, 2015)

Very well said! Greenwich has given us a good summary of 21st century skills and capacities. Yes, Socrates would be pleased, but now we have our smart phones, our iPads, other tablets and virtually unlimited access to the wealth of knowledge beyond the agora, where Socrates held forth, visible from the rocky pathway leading up to the Parthenon in Athens.

But how do we know they're getting better at any of these laudable goals? This is, in part, the rationale for *Moving from* What *to* What If?

Authentic Achievement

Another primary reason for undertaking this project is the conviction that productive curriculum development, instruction and achievement today will be characterized by what Fred Newmann and his associates called "authentic achievement."

That is:

> intellectual accomplishments that are worthwhile, significant,
> and meaningful, such as those undertaken by successful adults:
> scientists, musicians, business entrepreneurs, politicians, crafts
> people, attorneys, novelists, physicians, designers and so on.
> (1996, p. 26)

Toward these ends educators will challenge students to "organize, synthesize, interpret, explain, or evaluate complex information in addressing a concept, problem, or issue" (p. 29).

Thus, my initial thrust has been to find educators at the secondary school level who exemplify these authentic problem-based, pedagogical principles and who are keenly interested in observing students' growth in the 21st century skills and capacities described below.

Even before ever encountering Magdalena Jenni's stark contrast between education in Germany—problem-based—and that in her host school—multiple-choice based—we were in search of those educators who were more in tune with how she learned back home.

Problem-based Learning

Significant for the content will be the curricular framework I have observed over the past decade and more, that is, problem-based learning. What I see in the several educators from different subjects are ways of challenging students to think, to analyze ill-structured, problematic, often open-ended situations; conduct purposeful, appropriate research; draw reasonable conclusions; and, upon occasion, respond to questions and feedback from instructors and peers.

What this means is that teaching and learning can and should be focused on confronting and engaging complex, ill-structured tasks that can be found in our lives beyond school:

> learning should be organized around authentic problems and projects that are frequently encountered in non-school settings. (Bransford, 2000, p. 77)

In humanities these situations/scenarios may involve the need to identify a problem area within our community; analyze it; figure out how to go about resolving it using a wide array of resources; analyze data critically; pose significant questions of resource persons (those in authority); share your findings with local community members—e.g. directors of the local shopping mall, hospital personnel/athletic directors and the like. Propose solutions, receive feedback and modify as necessary.

In physics a problem might involve using basic principles to redesign a local elementary school playground.

In biology it might involve designing a livable domed habitat out in the desert.

In math the challenge might be to design an ideal community using demographics from a given metropolitan area using principles of mathematical reasoning.

In language arts we may be challenging students to write their own biographies after reading Richard Wright's *Black Boy*.

In both humanities and sciences, students are being challenged to ask researchable questions; e.g. determine runway length for maximum airplane liftoff and how to prevent a country in civil war from devolving into total chaos.

Within this problem-based framework each educator models for us the creation of rigorous, high-intellectual-level challenges which require students to think productively, not merely memorize stuff to deposit on the teacher's desk on a Friday exam. In *Pedagogy of the Oppressed*, Paolo Freire (2000) referred to this as "the banking concept" of education—take in information and store it untouched until the need for a confirmatory withdrawal.

Assessment of Students' Progress

Thus, having begun this journey to observe and learn from explorers of excellence in education, I found myself immersed in what developed as a most vigorous social debate: how to evaluate teachers. We are always being evaluated by our supervisors, but with the onset of Common Core State Standards and the assessment of students' progress using standardized tests, we encounter a debate that should be occurring.

We should not be trying to figure out how to evaluate a teacher's performance using tests designed to assess students' skills and understandings in reading and math. We should be challenging all educators to create their own assessments of 21st century skills—see the Greenwich "Vision," again—and using this data to share with students, faculty, administrators, parents and the community.

I did not undertake this adventure in order to find superlative educators who raise standardized test scores.

No, our purpose here is to find models of excellence who follow in Socrates' footsteps: to "infect people with the same perplexities" about life he experienced.

Data Collection

And within this framework educators do have various ways of collecting data: pre/post assessment benchmarks; written journals in a One-to-One school; close observations of students engaged in problem solving; students' projects/products; interviews by teacher and author (Skype and in-person); classroom observations; and teacher reflections.

Therefore, in each chapter dealing with these skills we will present specific students' responses to benchmark tests, pre and post. You will find hard before and after data in Chapter Three, "Developing Abstract Reasoning," Chapter Five, "Enhancing Inquiry," Chapter Nine, "Playgrounds of the Mind," Chapter Ten, "Critical Thinking about Social Issues," and Chapter Eleven "Reasoning about Nature." You will find illustrative examples in Chapter Seven, "Nurturing Imaginative Behavior."

In each case you will encounter what I've called a Reflective Pause, an opportunity for the reader to analyze data herself before reading about the teachers' or author's own analyses. This approach deliberately interrupts the reading in an attempt to foster your own reflections on information presented.

In Chapter Three, "Developing Abstract Reasoning," we will begin to examine some of this student work, for example, their responses to tests of cognitive development, specifically the Peel Test of Contingency Thinking.

What do you think is the value of our having student data that is immediate, direct (not from standardized tests)? How can such information benefit our instructional processes and advise students, teachers, administrators, parents and the community?

Inquiry

Posing and pursuing substantive questions is how we learn about the world and how we can live more equitable lives together as different cultures. Inquiry plays a significant and different role within each subject. We will see it, for example, in the problem-posing and resolving in Sandusky civics projects as well as in the summative projects (Exhibitions) at The School of the Future where one student will ask,

> How does the radius of a loop-the-loop on a roller-coaster affect the height that a cart has to travel from in order to fully complete the track?

We will also note in certain classes (physics, language arts and social studies) how teachers have structured their demonstrations, problem solving and debates so that students have significant time to question each other. This peer-to-peer inquiry facilitates investigation in ways we have yet to determine.

And, we will find inquiry driving a history class backwards, from initial examination of the Crimean situation (a model of tension, perhaps) and the questions students pose in order to understand Ukrainian/Russian relations way back to 1917.

Unifying Experiences across Disciplines

One theme I have stressed to each of the participants in this study is our need as researchers, teachers and authors to uncover for ourselves the common threads/principles/ideas that unify what each one is doing in his or her classroom.

Here are several of those elements:

1. 21st century skills of reasoning are woven throughout the curriculum, manifesting themselves not only in the pre and post benchmarks but throughout the instructional process.

   For example, in First Grade we begin asking students to give reasons for their choices. This is the very same process we observe when making an argument in humanities as well as in physics and biology where young scientists are challenged to analyze data on plant growth or the effectiveness of cinnamon or garlic in killing bacteria and "make a claim giving good reasons and evidence," not merely present the correct answer.

2. Problem-, inquiry-based focus of instruction: not merely sitting back taking in facts, but trying to figure out a complex array of statistics involving the police in our community.

3. Focus on authentic challenges and tasks of high intellectual challenge: not memorizing stuff but asking hard questions about causes of the Ukrainian conflict.

4. Instructional approaches that evidence:

   Openness to inquiry, where each student is encouraged to pose meaningful questions in the pursuit of mastery and understanding;

   Modeling (using pendula, or poetry to represent key elements within our subject);

   Opportunities for students to make choices about content, means of researching and sharing understandings;

   Peer-to-peer critique, tutoring and direct teaching;

   Using varied ways of representing our thinking and conclusions: words, diagrams, formulas, equations, art works, not only words in declarative sentences;

   Multiple means of expressing meaning and understanding, be it in physics demonstrations of force, mass and acceleration, or on meanings and motives in *Our Town*;

   Opportunities for application to life situations beyond school;

   Reflections on content meaning and personal growth.

Elements of students' choice within each of the foregoing reflect the all-important element of control, personal control exercised over one's own educational processes.

Part of what makes these educators' learning experiences authentic is their challenging students to make their own decisions, a very apt preparation for life outside and beyond school.

These elements I hope will help the science and math teachers communicate with the literature, social studies and music/art teachers.

Argonauts of Educational Change

Each chapter in this book is designed to show how several educators have challenged students to think through authentic, more open-ended problematic situations in accordance with their own philosophies of education for a changing world, various local, state and national standards as well as very high level standards for 21st century skills from their own district:

♦ Tim Obergefell, Social Studies/Government, Pearson High School, Sandusky, OH

- Laura Mourino, Mathematics, Harvest Collegiate School, NYC

- Andy Snyder, Social Studies, Harvest Collegiate School

- Hannah Magnan and Sue Steidl, Language Arts, large suburban district

- Mike Zitolo, Physics, School of the Future, NYC

- Joshua Hurley-Bruno, Biology, School of the Future, NYC

- Beth Krone, Language Arts, Harvest Collegiate School, NYC

- Katy Snyder, Physics 1 and 2, Colorado Springs, CO

- Stephen Lazar, Social Studies, Harvest Collegiate School, NYC

- David Sherrin, Social Studies, Harvest Collegiate School, NYC

- Michael Duncan, Superintendent, Pike County Schools, Zebulon, GA

- Hannah Cebulla and Madie Kelley, Bozeman High School and now Montana State University undergraduates

- Francesca Harrison, graduate of School of the Future, Smith College

Some of these educators belong to the New York Performance Standards Consortium, a group of over thirty schools that develop their own rigorous assessments of students' progress, assessments that reflect college-level work, are ill-structured, authentic and demanding of intensive problem solving and critical analysis (http://performanceassessment.org, accessed December, 2015).[2]

Each of the educators in this study is an argonaut on the seas of change helping all the Sabrinas in our classrooms realize they can make a difference in this world.

It's our challenge to help them launch their ships, provide them with all the navigational aids they might need in order to reach those distant shores, territories resplendent with opportunities for personal and professional growth in ways that are enriching and contribute to the advancement of civilization.

Conclusion

The Ottawa-Carlton School District in Ontario noted that students now have access to virtually unlimited amounts of information at their finger tips "instantaneously."

Our job is to enable these students to know what to do with all this information.

They will not attain their own personal goals nor achieve esteemed citizenship unless they can sort the wheat from the chaff, identify good reasoning from the lack thereof, challenge authorities who make unsupportable claims and can identify significant problems within our society and work toward their resolution.

Application

1. Who are the Sabrinas in your classes?

2. How are you challenging them to achieve efficacy and a sense of self-determination and responsibility?

3. To what degree do your units of instruction challenge students to engage in complex, rigorous and authentic intellectual work, involving inquiry, problem solving, critical/creative and reflective thought?

4. What does your school/district mission statement call for in terms of students' future behavior? To what extent do you agree/disagree with the Greenwich, CT, "Vision of the Graduate" where the first goal is for students to be able "to pose and pursue substantive questions" and conduct investigations with appropriate problem-solving, critical/creative/reflective thought processes?

5. To what degree do you attempt to assess these behaviors?

6. In your own classroom which 21st century skills are at the heart of your curricular units? Which ones do you assess and how?

7. For a future unit, identify the major intellectual skills and capacities you wish to focus upon. What kinds of problem-based learning experiences will you present to your students?

Notes

1. I've told this story elsewhere: *Quest for Antarctica—A Journey of Wonder and Discovery* (2007).

2. For sample performance assessments, see: http://performanceassessment. org/consortium/cfaq15.html. The schools represented within this study, School of the Future and Harvest Collegiate, are multi-ethnic, with large percentages of free and reduced lunch. The former school has a graduation rate over 95%.

References

Arendt, H. (1977) "Reflections," *The New Yorker*, 5 December.

Bransford, J. (2000) *How People Learn—Brain, mind, experience, and school.* Washington, DC: National Academy Press.

Freire, P. (2000) *Pedagogy of the Oppressed.* London: Bloomsbury Academic.

Newmann, F., & Associates (1996) *Authentic Achievement—Restructuring schools for intellectual quality.* San Francisco, CA: Jossey-Bass.

Chapter 2

Curricular Framework for Authentic Learning and Assessment

In this chapter, we will focus on how to fashion long-range curricular units that will embed within them the kinds of intellectual challenges necessary for success within any endeavor in our professional and personal lives.

Yes, we can plan a great problem-solving or critical thinking lesson as a one-time-shot for Monday or Tuesday, but how do we make such skills the major challenge for our students for an entire unit, composed of many lessons leading up to certain culminating experiences?

We will have no sustained growth if we exercise our biceps or leg muscles sporadically, on random occasions. Such physical development, like our mental development, needs to be planned out in advance and sustained over time.

"Macbeth Activities"

We don't usually think of curriculum development in Shakespearean terms, but there are similarities.

I have taught *Macbeth* on several occasions both in urban and suburban schools. It's always a rigorous challenge primarily because of the intense story of "vaulting ambition" crushed on the rocks of despair.

I've loved teaching about the language Macbeth uses at the end of his life as he sees the forces of good arrayed against his dirty deeds:

> Out, out, brief candle!
> Life's but a walking shadow, a poor player,
> That struts and frets his hour upon the stage,
> And then is heard no more. It is a tale
> Told by an idiot, full of sound and fury,
> Signifying nothing.
>
> (Act 5, sc. 5)

How I loved introducing students to these Shakespearean metaphors: "walking shadows" and "poor players." Sounds rather grim. But Shakespeare has painted such a telling portrait of an overly aggressive leader who falls from the weight of his own guilt.

Other Shakespearean characters, of course, are more illuminating:

But soft! What light through yon window breaks?
It is the east and Juliet is the sun.

What does Macbeth have to do with curriculum planning?

Just this shared wisdom from David Perkins of Harvard's Project Zero. He once suggested to me that so much of what he saw in classrooms seemed to him like what he called "Macbeth activities": "full of sound and fury signifying nothing."

Meaning there was a lot going on, but they failed to add up to significant learnings.

A principal in a South Carolina elementary school made a similar comment during a workshop once. "I love seeing all the children's art works, their projects and so forth. But I'm never sure what they represent in terms of students' learning. What do they all add up to?"

In other words, have any of them been planned as learning experiences culminating a unit of instruction during which students had certain learning outcomes? No, we do not wish to overly program and limit our students' thinking so that we can predict with precision what they will know and be able to do. There will always be room for those unintended learnings, the ones that surprise us with their originality and ability to reveal just how our students think and feel by asking, "what is fascinating you here?".

More Rigorous Planning

We can consider long-range planning involving authentic learning, inquiry and rigorous assessment as a drama played out in several acts. Like any playwright a curriculum planner has to know what the play will be about. Aristotle in *The Poetics* writes about the essence of drama, what he calls the "action." This concept guided me as a young English teacher, and I referred to Francis Fergusson's *(The Idea of a Theater)* explanation of the action as that which "the dramatist is trying to show us" through plot, characterization, language and thought. In *Macbeth*, the action would seem to be to become King and, thereby, attain power. (Fergusson, 1949, p. 244)

Figure 2.1

Inputs	Processes	Outputs
Curricular Frameworks, CCSS, C3, NGSS		Students' Growth in Skills, Understandings
Goals, Objectives		Dispositions
Teacher Abilities	**Authentic Learn-ing Experiences**	Thinking Skills
Students' Capabilities/ Interests		Understandings
Parental Priorities/Needs		Unintended Outcomes/ Hidden Curriculum
Multiple Resources/ Technologies		
Open/Inquiry Environment		

For a novel like *Catcher in the Rye*, Salinger's major action might be thought of as preserving and protecting childhood innocence by being the person who catches children in the fields of rye before they fall over the cliff into the phoniness and nastiness of adulthood.

The same is true in designing educational experiences, especially if we wish to avoid the Perkins' observation about "sound and fury signifying nothing."

All our planned experiences need to add up to meaningful learnings and capabilities (to write, compute and think) as much as possible. If we can focus our intentions upon that which is most important for students to learn, we can then organize all the learning experiences toward that end.

Curricular Frameworks

Here in Figure 2.1 we have, I hope, a simple way of blocking out the dramatic action to take place on the stage of our classrooms. We're looking at establishing authentic learning experiences, derived from our core standards and subject matter priorities (in terms of important concepts and ideas) that will result in students achieving lasting understandings as well as demonstrating growth in the all-important processes of thinking and figuring things out.

Inputs are those factors/elements we consider in planning for meaningful learning. In this case we are working within traditional curricular frameworks (and their revision by Wiggins & McTighe, 1998). This is the Tylerian framework, one that has governed curriculum development ever since Ralph Tyler first proposed it for his own curriculum course at the University of Chicago in 1949 (Tyler, 1949):

1. What educational purposes should the school seek to attain?

2. How can learning experiences be selected which are likely to be useful in attaining these ends?

3. How can learning experiences be organized for effective instruction?

4. How can the effectiveness of learning experiences be evaluated?

For years we have used this framework whenever planning units or the lessons therein:

1. What are our intended student outcomes? What do we want students to be able to know, do and be at the end of instruction? That is, they should know basic facts, concepts and principles in all our subjects, but, more significantly, be able to use them to solve authentic problems, not merely recite them on Friday.

2. What learning experiences will move us toward these ends?

3. How do we organize them? That is,

   a. What kinds of provocations can we use *to initiate* instruction, the problematic scenarios that will invite students to participate, grab their attention, give them a buy in by challenging them to raise significant questions?

   b. *Core learning* experiences—direct teaching investigations to answer questions, small group problem solving, critical analysis, drawing conclusions.

   c. *Summative experiences* wherein students demonstrate their understandings before authentic audiences.

4. How do we know students have gotten better at understanding complex concepts and ideas as well as improving in their thinking abilities?

Within this framework we can integrate all those important processes, skills and capacities outlined within the common core and other subject matter standards.

Thanks to the excellent work of Grant Wiggins and Jay McTighe (1998), we have revised this Tylerian framework to place more emphasis upon ensuring that we plan for meaningful assessments from the very beginning. This was probably part of Tyler's original concept, that we should consider our intended outcomes and how to assess them at the outset. That is, we should know beforehand how we would assess their abilities to solve civic problems in Sandusky, OH, or complex social issues confronting the nation, like uses of food stamps.

What evidence will we gather in order to demonstrate students' understandings? We shall throughout this book be referring to benchmark assessments to help us identify students' strengths and needs for improvement in terms of their abilities to think through complex, authentic problematic situations.

The Curricular Drama

Act One: What's this unit about?

Identify those concepts, ideas, skills, dispositions within your subjects that are important for students to consider over time and in depth. To be found within common standards (CCSS, C3, NGSS, district 21st century criteria); the needs of each discipline, of society and the interests of students.

Concepts should be Robust within subject and possess one or more of the following (Figure 2.2):

a. Integrative Significance—Connected to many other key concepts, like equality, revolution, systems, choice, cell, congruence, balance of forces (physics and history), self-direction and control.

b. Analytic Power—Can be used to analyze complex phenomena in one or more disciplines, e.g. critical reasoning, close reading, hypothesizing . . . finding corroborating sources . . .

c. Historical/Societal Importance, e.g. revolution, individual rights, communicable diseases, universal health care, imperialism, divine right of monarchs . . .

d. Logical Significance, e.g. understanding fundamental processes of algebra (factoring), geometry (congruence), language arts, sentence/paragraph construction.

In other words, which concepts in your subject are worth thinking deeply about, attaining a degree of deep and "enduring" understanding about?

Figure 2.2 Concept Map

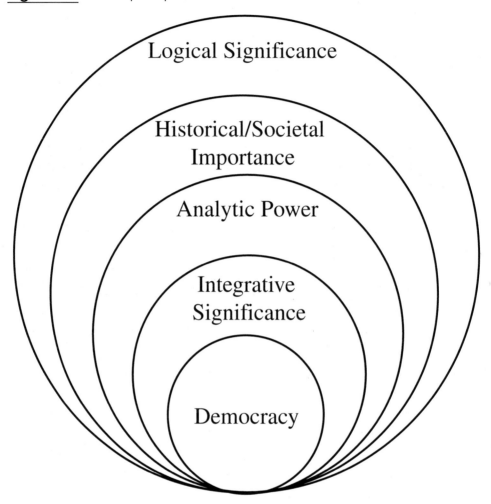

These need to be carefully selected (and have been by subject matter specialists) for they will form the core or thread for all learning experiences, especially our problematic scenarios and final assessments.

Skills will be drawn more directly from CCSS, C3, NGSS and the like, e.g.:

[Citing] strong and textual evidence to support an analysis of what a text says. (CCSS-ELA-Literacy RL 9–10.1)

Determine a theme or central idea and analyze its development over the course of the text. (RL 9–10.2)

Listen to or read the arguments of others, decide whether they

Make sense and ask useful questions to clarify or improve the arguments [in math]. (Ellenburg, 2015)

See Figure 2.3, Three Story Intellect, especially Levels II and III.

Act Two: What are the students going to be able to do?

Identify specific learning outcomes, "Students should be able to . . ." Here we want to stress students' gaining deep understandings of the most important concepts, for example, cell, revolutions, systems, friendship, democracy and equality/balance . . .

The importance of such considerations cannot be overstressed. Too often we get to the end of a unit and have little specific idea about what students should be able to do: plot and explain a force diagram for a body at rest on an inclined plane; compare and contrast Walter and George in *A Raisin in the Sun*, giving good reasons and evidence from the text; or make a proposal to local government officials for improvement of sports facilities in town.

On the other hand, we ought not to be so restrictive in these objectives as to overly limit students being able to make sense of the content in their own ways, explore new avenues of understanding and personal expressiveness.

How do we do this? By relying more upon Levels II and III of the Three Story Intellect: "Explain . . . analyze . . . compare/contrast . . . imagine . . . judge . . . apply . . . create a product."

Here is where we challenge students to "act upon" (Piaget) the stuff they are learning to construct their own meanings.

You will note that Figure 2.3 looks like an expansion of Bloom's Taxonomy of Cognitive Objectives.

Level I refers to those mental operations required for intake of information, Describe, List, Observe.

Level II focuses upon those mental processes required to do something with the information, pose and solve a problem, explain, think critically. Our objectives need to emphasize these more demanding requirements, otherwise we will task students with taking in and simply regurgitating information. To be learned and understood it must be processed, worked over, thought about, mulled over.

And then Level III helps us go beyond given information with questions such as those you will find in several of the scenarios presented here, "What if?" imagining what goes beyond the text or what's given, or applying learned lessons to one's own experiences.

Figure 2.3   Three Story Intellect

Level III: Applying/Using Knowledge to Demonstrate Understanding

Evaluate
Judge
Imagine
Speculate . . . if . . . then
Estimate
Apply a principle
Forecast
Create a product

Level II: Processing Information (in order to understand)

Compare/contrast
Classify
Identify variables
Analyze
Distinguish cause and effect/fact and opinion
Pose problems, generate solutions and solve
Make decisions
Infer and draw conclusions
Hypothesize, experiment and draw conclusions
Explain why, justify decisions/conclusions

Level I: Gathering Information

Describe	Name
Observe	Recite
Record data	Recall

Source: Fogarty, Robin J. Problem-Based Learning & Other Curriculum Models for the Multiple Intelligences Classroom. Copyright © 1997 by Corwin Press. Reprinted by permission of SAGE Publications, Inc.

For example, within a study of the US Constitution we might have these three different levels of intended outcomes:

Level I: Describe the development of The Bill of Rights.

Level II: Select those amongst the ten first amendments that you deem most relevant today, explaining why. Be sure to relate each to a current and significant issue and explain why you think each is important. Compare/contrast and draw your own conclusions giving good reasons and evidence.

Level III: Were there to be a constitutional convention, which of the first ten amendments would you modify and why? Or which might you add and why?[1] Cite historical reasons for the amendment as well as current thinking about ways to improve thereupon. How might you advise a new democracy (in the developing world) to ensure the human rights of all citizens?

Once we have our intended outcomes it is far easier to plan for assessment of same.

Act Three:[2] How many and different ways are there to learn/acquire deep understandings?

Map out a wide variety of learning experiences to achieve these intended outcomes, including those characterized by:

Challenges from each level of the Three Story Intellect

Complexity

Meaningfulness for students—that is, connected to their own lives

Opportunities for individual as well as collaborative problem solving and critical thinking

Access to multiple resources and technologies

Opportunities to make choices . . .

One way to conceptualize a unit program is with these three major elements:

Initiating Experiences: Problematic situations (including benchmarks), provocations and other complex situations that will foster analysis and inquiry, leading to

Core Learning Experiences, most characterized by:

Choice and students' shared control

High interactivity, small group peer problem solving

Direct teaching of core concepts and ideas

Conducting purposeful research amongst multiple resources

Data gathering and critical analysis, further inquiry

Drawing conclusions

Sharing findings with authentic audiences, fellow students

Opportunities to respond to "What if?" analytic questions.

Summative Experiences: Final presentations, assessments, opportunities for feedback on students' work and improvement. Reflections on process.

Act Four: How will we empower students and invite inquiry?

Brainstorm a variety of assessment experiences, both pre and post, that will obtain benchmarks for students' abilities, knowledge and understandings.

For example, to assess students' abilities to analyze experimental data and draw reasonable conclusions, we give them the Alka-Seltzer Rocket challenge (Chapter Eleven, "Reasoning about Nature"): How many milligrams of A-S will it take to send a toy rocket highest?

For Mike Zitolo this is his first benchmark, an assessment that tells him to what extent his students can analyze data, and draw conclusions giving good reasons and evidence.

Problematic Scenarios

Another approach is to craft what I have called a problematic scenario (see box below), a situation that invites inquiry, problem solving and critical thinking and may also be used as a summative assessment.

Here are teacher-crafted problematic scenarios designed to foster inquiry as well as serve as final summative assessments:

1. You are a meteorologist charged with explaining the water cycle . . .

2. You are a planner responsible for redesigning our playground . . .

3. You are responsible for helping rebuild New Orleans (after hurricane Katrina) . . .

4. You are responsible for finding ways to solve problems of ocean pollution . . .

5. You are the owner of a factory with responsibility to design a solution to this current problem . . .

6. You are responsible for designing an ABC book on Land Forms . . .

7. You must prevent a pyroclastic flow from destroying your town . . .

8. You are responsible for designing a habitat on Mars . . .

---

9. You are an advisor to Apple's Tim Cook to design a new "Think Different" poster for the iPhone

10. You are responsible for designing an improved roller-coaster for the theme park . . .

11. You are the owner of prime land on Lake Erie and will plan for its recreational use to stimulate local economy . . .

12. Assess the needs of an African nation, plan solutions, make application to the World Bank . . .

13. You are responsible for (a) preventing concussions during football teams' games; (b) Designing/funding/constructing outdoor basketball facilities; (c) Preventing accidents in front of McDonald's at the Mall (Sandusky, OH) . . .

14. You need to decide: whether to drop the atomic bomb; how to keep colonies within the British Empire . . .

15. You are a biographer researching 19th century novelists (e.g. Woolf, Dickens, Crane, and Melvilte . . .) and will explore how their world views would affect their analyses of current problems/writings . . .

16. You must determine the extent of bacterial contamination, make recommendations . . .

In each scenario we have:

Significant concepts central to the unit and the curriculum.

Challenges to engage students intellectually at Levels II and III, that is to think: identify and solve problems, make decisions, think critically/ creatively and reflectively.

Relevance to their lives sufficient to spark interest.

Opportunities to "pose and pursue substantive questions."

Opportunities to play the role of an important decision maker within the complexities of the situation.

Each scenario is sufficiently open-ended in order to challenge students to become close observers, gathering data, to relate to prior knowledge and to ask good questions that can then be used together with the teachers' leading or guiding questions. These scenarios provide not only a provocation to stimulate interest, but they also foster inquiry and can be used as one of the summative assessments for the unit. (See Chapter Five, "Enhancing Inquiry," and Chapter Seven, "Nurturing Imaginative Behavior.")

Act Five: How do we know they've gotten better?

Students and educators self-assess outcomes using pre-determined ways of evaluating students' growth:

Bench mark tests: Pre, Formative and Summative Assessments (including problematic scenarios). Re-administer the same or very similar benchmarks to assess the extent and quality of students' growth. See Chapters Three through Eleven where you will find specific benchmarks, students' responses and teachers' evaluations of their work. You will also find there the controlling rubrics guiding students' work and development of their thinking.

Students will conclude a unit's work by completing the challenges presented in the problematic scenarios:

1. Make your presentation to the World Bank on recommendations for economic growth of an African nation.

2. Present your plan for controlling bacteria within the school.

3. Complete and share your research on the extent of sexual assaults in college demonstrating your ability to think mathematically/statistically (an additional authentic assessment in algebra).

In each of these presentations students and teachers can determine the quality of thinking and understanding of major concepts through students' spoken and written words. When there are opportunities for a panel of "experts" to review students' work, they will ask the most important kinds of questions, the "What if?" conditional thinking questions that test a student's understanding of relationships amongst the significant variables.

In Mike Zitolo's Physics 1 class Charmain presented her research on the optimum length of a take-off runway at LaGuardia Airport in NYC for a Boeing 777. I saw her pause with each of Mike's questions, reflect on what she had already done, make tentative drawings and calculations on the white board and, finally, generate a response that more than adequately demonstrated her understanding of the complex aerodynamics involved with this aircraft.

These "What if?" questions are perhaps one of the best ways for us to determine the extent and quality of students' understanding. I was also present when these kinds of questions on a Capstone Project[3] caused Mike and his team to tell the student that she needed to try again next semester, which she, of course, did.

We will, of course, continue to use traditional means of evaluating students' learnings and understandings. Recent research (Paul, 2015) presents evidence of the efficacy of frequent quizzes to test our memories for recently ingested facts and concepts. This would be at Level I of the Three Story Intellect. Somewhat surprisingly, "Retrieving is the principal way learning happens." (p. 57) This is more powerful for subsequent learning and achievement than the oft-used highlighting and re-reading notes. Furthermore, "The process of pulling up information from memory also fosters what researchers call deep learning," that which requires inferencing, making connections and applying what we know.

Process as Content

Years ago two authors, Parker and Rubin, wrote a seminal text, a very slim one at that, called *Process as Content* (1966). Their contention was that within all disciplines there are important intellectual processes that are to be considered as the content of that subject. For example,

> History—Critical analysis of original documents; construct a theory or model (from existing evidence) of what a Sumerian civilization might have been like. (Parker & Rubin, p. 38)

> Literature—Reason analogically about different characters in plays, novels and short stories. Draw conclusions with good reasons, corroborating evidence (show counter arguments) and conclusions.

> Mathematics—Ability to conduct statistical analysis of complex issues; derive and explain the slope of a line; solve systems of linear equations.

> Science—Observe phenomena in nature, ask questions, establish testable hypotheses and conduct experiments, draw reasonable conclusions.

In the Common Core State Standards we have, essentially, a set of significant intellectual processes we wish students to master. The choice of how to achieve these ends is up to the imagination of each teacher within a given district. These skills are neatly arrayed from simple to complex in both mathematics and language arts (Marzano et al., 2013, p. 18 ff). For example, becoming familiar with "Numbers and Quantity" and "Analyze how and why individuals, events and ideas develop and interact over the course of a text" (College and Career Readiness Standard 3, Reading, Marzano et al., 2013, p. 16).

This also means that when we want students to develop the skills of "constructing effective arguments and . . . using relevant evidence," it's up to us to design the instructional framework. In Andy Snyder's classroom, students engaged with such topical issues as Stop and Frisk in New York City; voting rights for young adults; and, the wisdom of cutting benefits in the Food Stamp program; making claims, citing counter claims and warrants for appropriate evidence.

In biology, Joshua Hurley-Bruno challenges students to conduct a lab to discover the effects of various spices, garlic, turmeric and cinnamon, on the growth of bacteria. The question one group of students designed was "How will a spice (garlic as compared with cinnamon, turmeric, cilantro or oregano) prohibit the growth of bacteria (as measured by the overall percentage of bacteria on a grid)?"

Some students thought garlic would be the main inhibitor. Others hypothesized it would be cinnamon. One student found cinnamon to be the major inhibitor, while others determined it to be oregano. Did they approach this challenge cold? No. They had already conducted some background readings in order to ground their hypotheses in research and theory.

These students were evaluated not only on their lab procedures and drawing appropriate conclusions about results, but also on their ability to pose a good "testable and specific" question, one that "clearly identifies a potential causal relationship between variables and states how the results will be measured." This is the heart and soul of doing good science—posing a substantive question we can answer.

Because Josh wanted to support his colleagues in other subjects (language arts), he is educating his young biologists to pay close attention to the strength of their argumentation. Hence the evaluative criteria challenging students to:

Identify whether or not the hypothesis is supported by data . . .

Craft a claim stating or reflecting on the results of the investigation . . .

Use relevant and analyzed data to support the claim . . .

Supply one possible explanation for the data . . .

Elaborate on the evidence/data . . .

Identify relevant sources of error and discuss their potential effects on the data . . .

(Personal communication, May, 2015)

There was, hence, more emphasis on argumentation and experimental design than what Josh called the "cookie-cutter" lab outline.[4] In such a report you would present and interpret data and state whether or not your hypothesis was confirmed.

When I delved more deeply into why Josh emphasized argument in biology, he told me:

Initially, the common core standards pushed me towards using more argument within science class. However, I now see it as an important tool for increasing student interest, pushing students towards deeper understanding of content/concepts and facilitating their understanding of the complex and significant issues surrounding the ideas we investigate. In addition, examining data and observing student growth in argumentative writing (and speaking) truly demonstrates the value of this work. Students just read their first discussion section (one area of argument in class) and were shocked at how much they have grown this year. (Personal communication, June, 2015)

What's key here is that Josh sees challenging students to engage deeply in analyzing, explaining the data, plus identifying sources of error and seeking possible applications beyond the experiment leads to deeper understanding of content.

Josh is constantly modeling this approach, using claims, reasons and evidence.

If the experiment turns out contrary to expectations, he's likely to ask students "to craft a claim outlining the occurrences in this lab . . . Support your claim with relevant and analyzed data." In other words, let's understand why our expectations were violated.

I once asked a college chemistry professor what a good chemist needs to be able to do. "Ask good questions," he responded.

"And how much time do we spend on developing their ability to 'ask good questions'"? I asked.

"Almost none," he replied. "There's no time."

There's no time if inquiry and critical reasoning are not priorities.

In social studies we are interested, with the C3 framework in social studies, in students' abilities to ask good questions about complex, ill-structured events. In Steve Lazar's classroom students posed such questions about the Crimean conflict early in 2014. They can then be evaluated on the quality of their questions as well as on their understanding of this crisis following the collapse of the Soviet Union and the end of the Cold War. (See Chapter Five.)

How scientists, historians, literary analysts, mathematicians, pictorial artists and linguists gain new knowledge is important enough for us to observe, monitor and record as growth.

"Process *is* content."

Making It "Real"

I once asked a group of middle school students how they would advise new teachers on engaging students' interests, keeping them highly engaged. Here's what they said: "Make it real."

Make the instruction relate to what goes on not only in their lives, but in the world at large.

What we hope and expect to experience in any theatrical offering is a drama reflecting how people live their lives. *All My Sons*, *Elephant Man*, *A Raisin in the Sun* and *Carousel* represent such dramatic events we have enjoyed.

One of the major themes of this book is how excellent teachers are challenging students to think through authentic, ill-structured problematic situations.

How do we craft such learning experiences?

1. Review the definitions above (Newmann and associates, 1996) of "authentic learning experiences" as that which adults engage in during their professional lives.

2. Design experiences that involve students in

   a. Posing and resolving problems

   b. Asking good questions and conducting purposeful research

   c. Making decisions

   d. Critically analyzing data, claims

   e. Imagining alternatives in the process of problem solving and critical analysis

   f. Hypothesizing, designing and implementing experiments

   g. Drawing reasonable conclusions

   h. Creating original works of art for purposes of functional design, personal expression. (See Levels II and III of Figure 2.3, Three Story Intellect.)

3. Find provocations, illustrations, problematic scenarios, conflict situations that require *judgment*, *innovation* and use of knowledge and skill. Ask students to "do" the subject.

   Replicate contexts in which adults are "tested" in the workplace, in civic and personal life.

   Allow appropriate opportunities to *rehearse, practice, consult resources and get feedback* on and refine performances and products. (Wiggins, 1998)

Examples: Analyzing and responding to these questions:

Respond to: "Should the Food Stamp program be cut substantially?"

Use physics principles to analyze children's movements within a playground.

Given the situation in Crimea what questions do we have and how can we find answers?

If you were to construct a biosphere in the desert of Arizona what variables would you have to consider and how would your plans take them into consideration?

Given these NYPD data on Stop and Frisk, what questions would you ask and how would you go about determining an answer?

Assume you are the leader of an African nation, how would you research, plan and implement designs to foster economic growth?

Analyze data for employment within a city, state or nation, organized by year, type of job, gender, race and salary. Draw conclusions and support with evidence.

Performing for Understanding

If an actor thoroughly understands a character, she will communicate the depths of this understanding through her entire performance. Superficial understandings, without imaginative background creation, will result in flat, one-dimensional portrayals where the actors, for want of being able to act in character, stand there moving their fingers around the edges of the desks and chairs.

Thanks to the work of the scholars at Harvard's Project Zero (David Perkins et al.) and to Grant Wiggins and Jay McTighe, we are all very sensitive to this concept of teaching for understanding. That is, focusing upon concepts and ideas that will provide the focus of their "enduring understandings."

The ability to speak and write knowingly about the concept of freedom both within an historical context of the American Revolution, the Arab Spring, and human rights abuses within many countries today, may be hallmarks of a deep understanding of that foundational concept.

Perkins and his colleagues write about "performances of understanding," and this is what we intend in using CCSS, C3 and NGSS. We want students to do more than recite facts or give scripted explanations for finding that the center of the earth is hot.

In order to plan for "performances of understanding," we can follow the three-step challenge framework above by:

1. Selecting key concepts and ideas from our multiple sources (frameworks designed by each district, subject specialists, International Baccalaureate . . .).

2. Identifying what we want students to be able to do at the end of instruction, our goals and objectives derived from CCSS and students' needs (to craft narrative writings . . . apply principles of trigonometry to physics problems of balance of forces).

3. For example with the concept of democracy we can challenge students to do the following on an upward scale of difficulty:

   a. Define the concept

   b. Give illustrations of democracies in other countries

   c. Explain its origins in history, in specific countries

   d. Compare the forms of government in two or more different countries, e.g. the United States and Italy, France, the United Kingdom, Turkey, Indonesia . . . and draw reasonable conclusions

   e. Create a model, metaphor or analogy for a democratic society

   f. Analyze one historical development of democracy to determine how its roots were different from that of any country mentioned in "d" above

   g. Determine the likelihood of democracy developing and flourishing in any one or two "developing nations"

   h. Respond to "What if?" conditional questions about potential events in existing or emerging democracies

   i. Take another point of view, e.g. What does our democracy mean to a member of the Taliban, to a member of Russia's governing parliament, to an Iranian?

   j. Teach the concept to students at least two grades earlier than yours.

These are various intellectual challenges that will test the depth of understanding of students about the concept of democracy. It is not, therefore, enough to establish depth and quality of understanding to ask for definitions, examples and explanations of various facets of living in a democracy. Creating models, analyzing historical developments, responding to "What if?" questions and teaching the concept are all possible ways of challenging students to demonstrate their "enduring understandings."

Conclusion

We have attempted in this chapter to demystify some of what curriculum planning with respect to common subject matter standards is all about.

We're using a tried and true curriculum planning framework, that of Ralph Tyler (1949) to help us conceptualize what a unit of instruction would look like, what the planning thereof would entail.

Most significantly, we need to focus on those concepts and ideas that are robust within the curriculum—have multi-layered significance, relationships and depth; identify the mental operations we wish students to engage in (finding evidence to support claims is one of the major threads running throughout the ELA standards, for example); and devise authentic, open-ended learning experiences that will invite inquiry, critical analysis and lead to well-planned summative assessment experiences that reveal students' depths of understanding.

Our focus throughout this volume is on long-range planning, units of inquiry that are comprised of different individual daily, weekly lessons.

All of which can, with forethought and good planning, result in evidences of students' growth over time.

To round out our Shakespearean dramatic motif for this chapter, Prospero ends *The Tempest* with

we are such stuff as dreams are made on . . .

Application

Sample Unit Plan In Accordance with CCSS—ELA

Note to reader: *Read the sample unit and pay attention to what you would consider the levels of intellectual challenge students will be engaged in. Are they reflective of what we have been calling "authentic intellectual work," problem-based learning, Levels II and III of Three Story Intellect? In other words, to what extent are we challenging students to engage in our 21st century intellectual skills required for success in the world beyond schooling?*

Act One

Topic/Concept: Struggle for Identity

> *Action:* To find or fashion one's identity
> (Integrative, Analytic and Historical Robustness)

> *Essential Question*: How do culture, history and family shape our emerging identities?

Skills/ Intellectual Processes:
CCSS ELA: Literacy 9–10:

1. Cite textual evidence to support a conclusion.

2. Determine a theme or central idea and follow development throughout text.

3. Analyze how complex characters develop and change over the course of a work of art. (9–10.1.2.3)

Primary Resource:

Richard Wright's *Black Boy*

Complementary sources:

James Joyce, *A Portrait of the Artist as a Young Man*

Annie Dillard, *An American Childhood*

Lorraine Hansberry, *A Raisin in the Sun*

Alice Walker, *The Color Purple*

Act Two

Intended Outcomes: By end of this four-week unit students will:

1. Analyze major characters in terms of perceived strengths/weaknesses, making comparisons to other characters in primary and other works.

2. Create illustration of major theme(s) within primary (or secondary) sources using any art form.

3. In both 1. and 2. above provide solid, relevant and recurring evidence from the text to support conclusions.

4. Demonstrate understanding of how authors use literary devices such as metaphor, irony, personification, symbolism and the like.

5. Create their own personal expression of identity.

6. Reflect on their own learning processes: What have you learned about yourself, about writing, about your culture?

Act Three

Possible learning experiences, not arrayed in special order:

Initial writing reflections on various passages

Dramatic readings and acting out

Listing all questions about primary sources, classifying, sorting and arranging by major concepts, use as guides for reading and discussion

Conducting Socratic Seminars, with inner and outer circles of discussants and observers analyzing characters within primary and secondary sources

Discussion and analysis of key concepts: identity; how environment affects character; use of literary devices—metaphor, personification, irony . . .

Writing workshops—critiquing texts providing substantive evidence

Using Twitter messages to various characters reflecting major thoughts/actions

Creating Identity Videos conveying your symbolic understanding of Identity within major works of literature, your own life . . .

Literary/Inquiry journals, kept daily with questions and students' responses, shared in class, driving discussions.

Act Four (possible assessments that might also serve as problematic scenarios and final assessments/benchmarks)

1. You are a newspaper editor reviewing two different books, *Black Boy* and *American Childhood/Color Purple*. Convey to your readership the essence of the identities (through actions) in both autobiographies. Pay close attention to all literary elements you deem important.

2. Compare and contrast two different passages, one from *Black Boy* and one from Annie Dillard's *An American Childhood*, for literary elements, style, tone and content. Demonstrate how each author's use of these literary elements enhances (or diminishes) characters' identities.

3. You are an historian writing a reflection on literature of identity of the latter twentieth century. Select any two or three books from our list to communicate to your audience life in America during this and earlier time periods. Be selective in your choice of representative selections paying close attention to the elements of culture, history and family and how they reveal characters' identities, both consciously recognized and unconsciously exhibited.

Each of these might serve as initial learning experiences, problematic-scenarios and pre assessment benchmarks, as complex, ill-structured and fostering inquiry kinds of experiences.

Sample benchmarks:

1. Analyze the first page of Wright's *Black Boy* for theme, major idea and literary devices that convey this theme (imagery, symbolism, metaphor/simile, personification). Be sure to present your reasons with evidence to support same.

2. Compare two paragraphs from the works of Wright and Dillard for theme, literary devices. Be sure to give your major conclusions, reasons and evidence.

Act Five

Use problematic scenarios (above) as pre and post summative assessments of major ELA 9–10.1.2.3 objectives.

Literary journals for growth in students' ability to question text and character, and other literary devices/formats.

Use any art form to depict your understanding of Wright's struggle for identity. Accompany with a well-crafted essay describing your thought processes, major sources of evidence to support your portrait of the artist. (For example, I once posed this challenge to college freshmen/sophomores in a World Literature course in college after the study of *Othello*.[5] To my astonishment, I received a detailed cartoon of Iago, a full-length poem of praise to Desdemona, and a marvelous sonata for viola on the themes of the entire play. Each artistic production was accompanied by an expository essay explaining the various elements within the cartoon, the poem and the sonata. Most other products were collages. (See eResources—history example.)

Consider your earlier planning and answers to this question: "What constitutes good evidence of conceptual understanding within the Essential Question—role of culture, history and family in fashioning our identities?"

Consider what evidence you will gather to reflect students' growth in:

Posing and pursuing a substantive question

Critically analyzing text using Claims, Reasons and Evidence, Counter Claims, Reasons and Evidence (see Chapter Ten).

Notes

1. In the past there have been advocates for amendments to ban flag burning, require a balanced amendment, repeal the *Citizens United* Supreme Court ruling and provide equal rights for all.

2. In my own thinking, it is possible to reverse Acts Three and Four: that is plan the initating experiences, the problematic scenario first, then plan out subsequent learning experiences. Here, I'm suggesting it might be easier to brainstorm learning experiences before identifying a good scenario to initiate inquiry for the entire unit. In either case, we will include inquiry, research and reporting experiences as part of the unit.

3. Required to pass on to the next level . . . required for graduation . . .

4. Other lab reports call for the following:

Discussion or Analysis
The Data section contains numbers. The Analysis section contains any calculations you made based on those numbers. This is where you interpret the data

and determine whether or not a hypothesis was accepted. This is also where you would discuss any mistakes you might have made while conducting the investigation. You may wish to describe ways the study might have been improved.

Conclusions

Most of the time the conclusion is a single paragraph that sums up what happened in the experiment, whether your hypothesis was accepted or rejected, and what this means (http://chemistry.about.com/od/chemistrylabexperiments/a/labreports.htm, accessed November, 2015).

5. Were I teaching this same unit now, I would lay out this challenge at the beginning of the unit, perhaps as a benchmark assessment: draw any character in literature to illustrate your understanding of who she/he was.

References

Ellenburg, J. (2015) "Meet the New Common Core," *The New York Times*, 16 June, p. A27.

Fergusson, F. (1949) *The Idea of a Theater—The art of drama in changing perspective.* Princeton, NJ: Princeton University Press.

Marzano, R. et al. (2013) *Using Common Core Standards to Enhance Classroom Instruction and Assessment.* Bloomington, IN: Marzano Research Laboratory.

Newmann, F., & Associates (1996) *Authentic Achievement—Restructuring schools for intellectual quality.* San Francisco, CA: Jossey-Bass.

Parker, J., & Rubin, L. (1966) *Process as Content.* New York: Macmillan.

Paul, A.M. (2015) "A New Vision for Testing," *Scientific American*, August, 55–61, 313, 2.

Piaget, J. (1964) "Development and Learning." In R. E. Ripple and V. N. Rockcastle (Eds) *Piaget Rediscovered.* Ithaca, NY: Cornell University.

Tyler, R. (1949) *Basic Principles of Curriculum and Instruction.* Chicago: University of Chicago Press.

Wiggins, G. (1998) *Educative Assessment: Designing assessments to inform and improve student performance.* San Francisco: Jossey-Bass.

Wiggins, G., & McTighe, J. (1998) *Understanding by Design.* Alexandria, VA: Association for Supervision and Curriculum Development.

Chapter 3

Developing Abstract Reasoning

Formal Operational Thinking

Betsy was a high school student in a history class I was observing in Ridge-wood, NJ. One day, during a unit on World Wars I and II, she raised her hand to ask this question: "Was Kaiser Wilhelm the Hitler of World War I?"

I was amazed at the question because I was at the time studying imaginative thinking in adolescents and was intrigued by her perceiving a multitude of possible ways in which these two leaders might have been quite similar.[1] Crossing generational boundaries, she was probably playing with the leadership characteristics of both men and wondering about their similarities and differences.

It is only recently that I realized that this on-the-spur-of-the-moment question might also reflect Betsy's quality of thinking, that she must have been engaging in what we call "Formal Operational" thinking as so labeled by Piaget (Inhelder & Piaget, 1958).

Our current project on intellectual growth was conducted in several high schools where students are adolescents and, therefore, should be capable of this more abstract reasoning capacity. This is a transition from reasoning primarily from concrete objects before us toward being able to think and reason with abstractions, considering multiple (two or more) variables at once, holding two constant and testing one, projecting imagined possibilities and laying out long-range plans for the future.

Formal operational thinking is important, I think, because we as secondary school educators may assume that all students are, because they are teenagers, competent when it comes to thinking abstractly, to reasoning with multiple elements or variables in mind, to projecting imagined consequences into the future, to imagining contrary-to-fact possibilities.

Such is not, however, the case.

How often have we seen students struggle with imagining life of a literary character?

With considering unseen possibilities, such as hidden assumptions, historical causes or literary character's motivations?

With reasoning about the comparative sizes of Earth, Mercury, Venus and Jupiter?

And having difficulty with direct and indirect proportions?

Not understanding the complexities of the concept of density, dependent upon mass, volume and pressure?

Students may struggle with abstract concepts, be unable to easily manipulate or compare one or more with each other. I'm sure that some of Betsy's classmates were surprised at her question and would not have been as comfortable playing with all those variables that she might have been tossing around in her mind that morning, or long beforehand.

Thus, it seems reasonable to attempt to gain insight into our students' thinking abilities in these foundational skills and processes.

Proportional Reasoning— Not Just in Math

According to Piaget, adolescents should develop an ability to engage in what he called "proportional reasoning." This process, most often evident in science and mathematical reasoning, involves comparing and relating multiple variables in our heads. Thus, we can understand how $a/b = c/d$. (You can see Betsy's analogy in similar terms. More below.)

There is some research claiming that only 50 percent of adults can reason proportionately (Lamon, 2005). This seems like a very high percentage of non-performance.

A proportional reasoning task in math might be the following: "Bob reads 60 pages in 30 minutes. How long will it take him to read 150 pages?"[2]

Similarly, which represents "a more significant change" in numbers: 3 children becoming 9 or 100 becoming 150?[3]

In physics, "the force of gravity between two masses is directly proportional to the product of the two masses and inversely proportional to the square of the distance between the two masses."[4]

In Humanities

But we can also challenge students in humanities to engage in finding relationships amongst two or more elements or variables:

History/social studies: how can we transform the scale of a map from 1" represents 5 miles to 3" represents x miles?

Compare the American Revolution to the War in Vietnam, the French and/or Russian Revolutions.

What kinds of relationships existed between Japanese movements and economic/military strategies in the Far East in the late 1930s and the US entry into World War II?

To what degree would you say that Macbeth's zeal for killing King Duncan was directly or inversely proportional to Lady Macbeth's prodding?

Proportional reasoning is a capacity we develop slowly, over time, and one that enables a wide variety of problem-solving abilities.

> We view proportional reasoning as a pivotal concept. On the one hand, it is the capstone of children's elementary school arithmetic; on the other hand, it is the cornerstone of all that is to follow. (Lesh, Post & Behr, 1988)

Figure 3.1

Simple tests to differentiate concrete from formal reasoning:

A. "If Kelly is taller than Ali and Ali is taller than Jo, who is tallest?" Students who must visualize, draw a diagram are probably thinking concretely.

B. "Third eye question." Asked where they would put a third eye on the human body, younger children, 9-year-olds, often replied, "On the forehead." A more original answer would be, "On the hand (11-year-olds) . . . back of the head."

C. Pendulum test. Show students how a pendulum works. Ask them to determine which variable (weight of pendulum, length of string, force of push) directly affected the speed of the pendulum swing. Students in the formal operational stage approached the task scientifically, that is, manipulating one variable at a time, holding the others constant. Younger children varied elements more at random and often got the wrong answer (www.simplypsychology.org/formal-operational.html, accessed May, 2015).

See Chapter Eleven, Mike Zitolo, Physics 1 for a discussion of this experiment.

"Careful Airman Test" of Contingency Thinking

We can infer our students' abilities with what scientists call "proportional reasoning" from their problem-solving abilities. But we can also give them a direct assessment.

Tim Obergefell analyzed students' cognitive development with a simple test devised by E.A. Peel called "The Careful Airman Test." Here is another challenge with no correct answer, but one that is designed to reveal our ability to recognize contingencies, options, alternative explanations.

> Only careful airmen are allowed to fly over high mountains. This summer a fighter pilot, flying over the Rocky Mountains, collided with an aerial sky ride cable and cut it, causing some sky ride cars to fall to the rocks below. Several people were killed and many others had to spend the night suspended above the rocks. Was this pilot a careful airman? Why do you think so? (Peel, 1974)

One of our students cited above responded thusly:

> No, the airman wasn't careful. He should've paid attention to his surroundings and been more aware of his surroundings. (A)

Another responded:

> I think this pilot wasn't very careful. He should know the area that he is flying around. He also shouldn't be flying too low to the mountains. Many different accidents could happen. I think that pilots should be trained before flying in dangerous areas. (B)

Whereas another one responded in this fashion:

> It would depend on the situation. This pilot could have been the most careful airman out there and still had a problem with seeing the lines or a problem with steering the plane. There could have been a failure with the plane engines and steering. The sky ride cables could have also been not seen because of a glare against the sun or could have been thinner so the pilot didn't see them. (C)

 ## Reflective Pause

Again, let us pause for your reflection on these three responses. What similarities and differences do you see amongst them?

The Peel Test was created to assess students' abilities to infer, to find possibilities and contingencies that are not explicitly stated. This is what reading specialists call "reading between the lines" to be able to draw reasonable inferences or conclusions. We take different pieces of information, relate them to what we already know—in this case, about flying, what causes accidents, human nature—and draw our conclusions.

We can see that students A and B are more or less controlled by the written word. There was an accident, he must have been careless. Whereas student C can analyze the complex, authentic and open-ended problem to see the possibilities: steering; engines; the glare of the sun.

One of the most complex, analytic thinkers in Tim's class is David:

> Despite the outcome of the situation, I believe that the pilot is a careful airman. This story does not describe the *weather conditions* the day of this accident, so it could have been storming, foggy, or cloudy. These conditions would have caused the pilot to *veer off course* and collide with the sky ride cable. Even the most cautious pilots are affected by unfortunate weather conditions, and the writer did not include that information in the paragraph. Also, this pilot was still very courageous and experienced as he was allowed to fly over the high mountains. (Emphasis added)

Of course, as we shall note further on in this volume, if a student progresses from being text-driven to seeing contingencies, this is a sign of growth, but we cannot necessarily attribute it to one teacher's class. There are too many other independent variables: the student's natural maturation; effects of other classes, peers and family.

We hope that between the administration of the Peel Test in September and in May, that students would move closer to the reasoning of David in Tim's class; that is, being able to perceive hidden contingencies.

But this does not always happen. Here's the post test of student A above:

> No, the airman was not careful because he ran into the sky ride cable. If he had been flying with caution he would have been on the look out for cables in the mountains, spotted it and avoided it . . . Perhaps the pilot was attempting to be courageous by flying through the mountains at a relatively low altitude. However, he was not careful as he was aloof enough to run into a sky-ride cable.

Here's student B's second take on the airman question:

> Only courageous pilots are allowed to fly over high mountains, but often courage comes at the cost of carelessness and safety. However,

we cannot be entirely sure if the pilot was careful or not, as we don't know the conditions of the crash. If it was dark out, or signal lights on the sky ride cars were out, then the pilot would simply not be able to see the ride against the mountain. If there were no cars in sight, maybe the cables were too thin to see from the airplane. While there are many situations where the pilot could be attentive and still crash, it is possible the pilot was just being careless after all. It is also a possibility that the pilot was not attentive, but that they would have crashed anyway if they were being careful.

What do you think of these responses? What kinds of change do you see in student B's response?

One of the objectives of a curriculum driven by authentic, more open-ended problems such as those described above and below is to foster this kind of contingency thinking, seeing the multiple possibilities that we conjure with our imaginations. Here is where Piaget's Formal Operations begin to become evident, during early adolescence for some students, but not all.

Reasoning in Mathematics—Algebra 1

Laura gave this benchmark test at Harvest/Collegiate School on 14th Street in Manhattan:

> Suppose that every hour of every day, an airplane leaves Los Angeles for New York City and at the same instant, an airplane leaves New York City for Los Angeles. Each flight takes 5 hours. In a single day, how many airplanes originating in New York City will pass airplanes originating in Los Angeles in the air?

"There are so many math variables within this problem," she told me as I struggled to remember how to analyze it.

Thus, in order to solve it her students needed to identify all the relevant variables and figure out the meaningful relationships amongst them—a good assessment of their ability to reason abstractly and manipulate several variables at once: locations; time of flight; take-off/landing times; hours in a day; simultaneity; number of airplanes; passing in mid-air (time/distance/location?).

One student, Wilette, drew a diagram, created a table and wrote this analysis, three forms of representation:

> There will be a total of 24 airplanes that pass each other because as it states "Every hour of every day" an airplane from LA and an airplane

from NY leaves. [Each takes 5 hours to make the cross-country journey.] So since it takes them the same amount of time to reach their destination and since they both leave every hour they will always be in the air at the same time. So because they leave every hour and there are 24 hours in one day there will be a total of 24 airplanes.

Reflective Pause

What does this test indicate about Wilette's abilities to reason abstractly?

This was, in fact, a concluding benchmark and we shall see in Chapter Nine how Wilette's reasoning improved from September to May— definitely exhibiting development of cognitive abilities, probably as the result of constantly being challenged with these kinds of authentic problems.

Reasoning about the Natural World

Physics

In introductory physics of Discovery Canyon High School, an International Baccalaureate school in Colorado Springs, Katy Snider's students are first asked, "What is necessary to design a good lab experiment?" Katy sent me the analysis of three of her students; High, Middle and Lower:

> The most important thing is to have a well developed problem and hypothesis. This allows for the consideration of lab materials and a procedure. We found that it was valuable to include units of measurement when discussing specific items or data. Also, one must consider adding a procedure that reveals something connected to the question/problem. (Andrew)
> When designing a lab, it is important not to have multiple variables in the lab. Also you have to describe everything in full detail so any person could attempt to do it. When writing the lab, specifics are also needed instead of being broad. (Jalan)
> When writing an experiment it is very important to make sure that what you are measuring is measurable. We realized that you can't measure the squishiness of a table, book, jacket or the floor. (JT)

"These responses came before we had any discussion of a well-designed lab or the rubric that I will be using," said Katy in an email (September, 2013).

Reflective Pause

Whose thinking seems to reflect enhanced, more mature complexity of thought? Why?

The lab rubric Katy uses includes these criteria:

1. A clear research statement is stated.
2. Relevant variables identified: dependent/independent.
3. Hypothesis: If . . . then . . . because.
4. In the procedure it should be clear how those independent variables are manipulated and explicitly mentioned how the control variables are kept constant.

It seems possible that the differences between the more complex and the more simplistic explanation might reflect differences in cognitive development, the ability in this instance to move beyond the immediate, concrete realities before us to manipulate in our minds different variables that are more abstract.

Of course, it is also probable that the differences between Andrew's more complex thinking and JT's more simplistic thinking, is a matter of previous involvement in designing and setting up lab experiments, in other words, a matter of prior experience.

IB Biology

Dr. Lanett Jauss teaches AP and IB Biology in North Kansas City, MO. She became interested in this research project because she had recently completed her doctoral studies on the degree to which one found evidence of higher order thinking amongst students in such advanced classes. One would think there would be solid evidence of same, but she did not find it.

One of her benchmark assessments concerns the kinds of research students would be studying during the coming year:

> Describe the differences between experimental and observational research. Then design an experiment to learn about "the effect of smoking on the lung capacity of women."

Here is Lanett's assessment of one of her students, Mark,[5] discriminating between experimental and observational research:

> Mark could identify both types of labs and the variables involved but when it came to giving an example for each kind both of his labs were experimental in nature not one of each. This shows me that the deep understanding of how to identify different types of scientific investigations is not fully developed. Since many scientists perform observational studies this is an important thought process as well.

Lanett's summative assessment of Mark:

> He is a hard worker, constantly needs attention, constantly checks to make sure he is "doing it right" or has the correct answer, lacks some confidence, caring, concerned, relies on memory quite a bit and at times does not have deep understanding so *does not remember information especially abstract concepts that can't be seen directly.* (Emphasis added)

Sounds as if he retains some characteristics of the thinker in the Concrete Operational Stage (Piaget). His need to be "doing it right" *may* reflect some discomfort with the ambiguity of complex thought and problem solving, "trying out different tracks" as Gilbert Ryle (1979) said, as one goes "exploringly" over new territory.

Classroom Discussions and Questions

Every action, every utterance, every penned word within a learning environment can be used as an assessment of students' knowledge, skills and attitudes. It goes without saying, I suggest, that all such information, including what we have described above, is inferential. That is, we are using words, spoken and written, art works of all sorts, with which to infer mental states.

All written work, classroom discussions and every product created by a student give us some indication of her subject matter knowledge, her ability to analyze situations and her attitudes toward that work.

Students' questions, for example, might provide us with excellent insight into their caste of mind, their ability to play with variables internally.

Let's return to Betsy in her favorite class, history, discussing World Wars I and II:

Was Kaiser Wilhelm the Hitler of World War I?

Her teacher paused a moment and then responded, "No, I wouldn't say that" and the class moved on.

 ## Reflective Pause

Look at Betsy's question. How would you as teacher have responded to her? What would you wish to determine about her thinking?

I was always intrigued by what characteristics of both she was comparing. Which was she not paying attention to and why?

Among those Betsy seemed to be considering were the following: leadership; command of the state; use of propaganda; building up armed forces; having visions of conquering all of Europe; strategic thinking; stance v. Great Britain; growing up in Vienna (Hitler). Maybe also the leader's history; education; proclamations (*Mein Kampf*); relationships with other heads of state . . . and so on.

With all of this, her posing the question might have been spur of the moment, but, on the other hand, she might have been mulling it over in her mind since the commencement of the World War II unit. I am now intrigued by how one goes about making such comparisons and the extent to which they might reveal abilities to engage in proportional reasoning: $a:b = c:d$.

Certainly there are so many possible variables here, that she could easily be manipulating a few significant ones in her mind while ignoring and/ or holding others constant. This is what we do when we create a scientific experiment: observe one variable while holding others constant.

What a treasure trove of reasoning possibilities in this question! What opportunities for in-depth discussions about leadership; Great Man in History theory; the wars themselves . . . !

Gravity on the Moon

Here's David's Ninth Grade science question: "What if there were no gravity on the Moon?"

The teacher entertained the question. "David's question. What do you all think?" What ensued was a lively discussion of possibilities, each of which could be tested with scientific precision. Again, consider all the possible variables: nature, effects of gravity; strength of gravity on the Earth and Moon; human mass/weight; relationships between the Moon and Earth (tides, gravity); orbit of the Moon; its composition, that of the Earth . . . And many more, I'm sure.

Unfortunately, when David's parents heard about this experience, one of them called the teacher to say, "My son has enough to learn in science that is factual without dealing in these kinds of hypotheticals."

Sadly, the teacher ceased posing what could be one of the best mind-stretching experiences his students would have, that is, posing "What if?" contrary to observations, hypotheticals that challenge us to conjure up possibilities, most of which could be tested in science. These hypothetical questions might also reveal students' abilities to imagine the unseen, the impossible, the contingencies that affect a given situation.

In history we pose these questions (e.g. "What if Truman had not dropped the bomb?"). The consequences cannot be tested rigorously, perhaps, but we still can use historical conditions from which to reason toward valid conclusions.[6]

Figure 3.2

Alternative means of determining qualities of cognitive development:

- The Peel Test of "The Careful Airman"
- Students' products:
  - Claims/wonderings/questions during discussions
  - Written work—analyses of complex phenomena/situations (historical circumstances; character developments in stories . . .)
  - Thinking/inquiry journals wherein students analyze data, complex situations
  - End projects that challenge them to engage in problem solving, critical analysis creative/innovative production

Thus, we are not constrained by pre, formative and summative assessments in our gathering of information about students' thinking and dispositions. All is potentially available for analysis. The benchmarks we have presented here are specifically designed for this analytic purpose.

Conclusion

What might become evident through these various assessments are the following generalities, true in many if not most cases:

A. All assessments have the *potential* for providing a representation of students' cognitive abilities. The more complex their answers are, for example, might be an indication of their abilities to think of and relate multiple variables in the abstract, imagine elements/factors not concretely present (Peel Test) and reason proportionately.

B. Every utterance from students is potentially an indicator of their foundational abilities to think abstractly, to analyze complex situations with many variables—think of Betsy's comparing Kaiser Wilhelm and Hitler and "What if there were no gravity on the moon?"

C. We must, however, be careful to compare the results of one assessment with other expressions of students' analyses of content. *One test does not provide us with conclusive evidence.* We can take one test as a *potential* indicator of cognitive differences.

D. Students' thinking at times is constrained by prior knowledge and experiences.

E. Their thinking may seem simple, naive, un-enhanced by being able to see contingencies (Peel Test), multiple possibilities, ways to effect change.

F. Their thinking may also be constrained by not knowing or having at hand the scoring rubric we are using.

Our students' cognitive developmental capacities develop over time. We should be aware of what they are currently and how to help them grow during our year or more with them.

Angler Fish

But beware of taking all of the foregoing too literally! What do you make of this question developed toward the end of a unit on ocean habitats taught within view of the Pacific Ocean? "Do you think that anglerfish think humans are fish sometimes?"

First of all, what is Jennifer doing here? Comparing humans with her favorite fish, the bottom-loving and rather ugly angler fish. She's also stepping out of her own skin to take the point of view of the anglerfish as it looks at humans.

When do we develop these abilities? During adolescence? Before?

Jennifer was in her first year of kindergarten at Mulgrave School in Vancouver (Barell, 2012) under the expert tutelage of Lorraine Redford.

As always, we should maintain healthy skepticism when considering students' words, especially so as not to underestimate them, as some claim Piaget did.

Application

1. How do you assess students' cognitive/intellectual development? We need not use the Peel Test, but should use current learning experiences to consider students' flexibility of thinking, their ability to consider contingencies, and to engage in abstract reasoning:

   Classroom discussions/questions/claims

   Written work

   End of unit/term projects

   Regular unit assignments calling for proportional reasoning/comparison contrasts and drawing reasonable conclusions

   Standardized tests like Peel's

   Creating verbal/written challenges calling for abstract reasoning:

   > "What if all the ice in Antarctic melted?"—Tim, a high school student responded quickly, "Venice would no longer be unique!" (Based on Torrance, 1966, 1974)

   > An alternative question: "Which two of these three are more alike and why—the American, French, Russian revolutions?"

2. How do you use this information to advise instruction and guide curriculum development?

3. What kinds of records do you maintain of students' benchmark performances? How might these assessments, like Laura's above, reveal potential cognitive capacities?

Notes

1. I described this project in *Playgrounds of Our Minds* (1980).
2. http://teachmath.openschoolnetwork.ca/grade-6/proportional-reasoning.
3. www.edu.gov.on.ca/eng/teachers/studentsuccess/ProportionReason.pdf.
4. Wikipedia, http://en.wikipedia.org/wiki/Proportional_reasoning.
5. "Mark" is a pseudonym chosen by the author.
6. When I first learned about David's question, I was writing *Playgrounds of Our Minds* (1980). This was before the publication of very challenging books such as Randall Munroe *What If?* (2014) and Niall Ferguson (ed.) *Virtual History* (2000).

References

Barell, J. (1980) *Playgrounds of Our Minds*. New York: Teachers College Press, Columbia University Press.

Barell, J. (2012) *How Do We Know They're Getting Better? Assessment for 21st century minds, K–8*. Thousand Oaks, CA: Corwin Press.

Ferguson, N. (ed.) (2000) *Virtual History: Alternatives and counterfactuals*. New York: Basic Books.

Inhelder, B., & Piaget, J. (1958) *The Growth of Logical Thinking from Childhood to Adolescence*. Abingdon, Oxon: Routledge and Kegan Paul.

Lamon, S. (2005) *Teaching Fractions and Ratios for Understanding* (2nd edn). Mahwah, NJ: Erlbaum. Quoted by Dole, S. in "Making Connections to the Big Ideas in Mathematics: Promoting proportional reasoning" (http://research.acer.edu.au/cgi/viewcontent.cgi?article=1086&context=research_conference).

Lesh, R., Post, T., & Behr, M. (1988) "Proportional Reasoning." In J. Hiebert & M. Behr (Eds) *Number Concepts and Operations in the Middle Grades*. Reston, VA: Lawrence Erlbaum & National Council of Teachers of Mathematics, pp. 93–118.

Munroe, R. (2014) *What If? Serious scientific answers to absurd hypothetical questions*. New York: Houghton Mifflin Harcourt.

Peel, E.A. (1974) "A Study of Differences in the Judgments of Adolescent Pupils." In Z. Cantwell & P. Svajian (Eds) *Adolescence: Studies in development*. Itasca, IL: Peacock Publishers.

Ryle, G. (1979) *On Thinking*. Totowa, NJ: Rowan & Littlefield.

Torrance, E.P. (1966, 1974) *The Torrance Tests of Creative Thinking*. Bensenville, IL: Scholastic Testing Service.

Chapter 4

Directing Goals toward Achievement

When I was fourteen years old I set down a goal in writing.

After having read several books on polar exploration, specifically those by Admiral Richard E. Byrd about his First and Second Antarctic Expeditions (1928–30, 1933–35), I wrote the following: "I hope that by the time I am fifty I will have been to Antarctica."

I fulfilled that goal when I was twenty-five, sailing to Antarctica on Byrd's flagship, *USS Glacier* (AGB-4) on two missions to McMurdo Sound during Operation DeepFreeze.[1]

It was when I became an educator years later that I reflected on this use of the future-perfect tense to capture what my imagination was driving me toward, visiting and exploring the southern continent, so full of mystery and fascination.

Goal-setting is touted by virtually every person writing about how to take charge of your own life, make it what you deeply wish it to be. Set a goal, write it down and keep it foremost in your mind every day. Some mavens even tell us to look in the mirror every morning, recite the goal, or have it affixed to a Post-it note right next to the mirror.

We're all familiar with teachers setting goals for our students: "Today, we're going to learn about the Amazon River Basin and how important it is to Brazil's economy." Or, more specifically, "Boys and girls, today we're going to learn how to write the introduction to a story."

What's different, of course, is that what we want to do is challenge students to look at their own work, decide what to do about it, set a goal for improvement. We're going to encourage them to take more control of their own learning both in and out of school.

It should be evident to all that what we want as a long-term goal for all educators is to set the stage for our students to be able to make decisions about their lives on their own, to be able to set their own priorities and with the help of friends, colleagues and relatives seek their fulfillment.

That was certainly true in my case. I set the goal at age fourteen, but needed encouragement and sage advice from grandparents, parents, teachers and Admirals in the Navy to fulfill it.

As one teacher said recently, "I want my students to be able to figure out these things on their own, when I'm not around to guide them."

The goal-setting I engaged in derived from polar explorers always having goals and specific objectives in mind: to be the first to reach the South Pole; to chart as much of the unknown from the air as possible.

Goal-setting like this reflects what Carol Dweck calls a "growth mindset," the self-confident belief that we can all improve, "get smarter," stretch ourselves into new areas of achievement (2007, pp. 16–17). This is the opposite of the fixed mindset: intelligence is a given, unchanging, and kids who are "smart" do not make mistakes. In other words, those with a growth mindset stretch themselves into areas where we all make mistakes, but where we can all learn.

To set a goal means we have a belief in the potency of our own self-development.

"Tell Your Parents"

I worked for several years with a math teacher in New Jersey who regularly challenged her students to examine their previous semester's work.

> Look at your final exams, your written work before that, at your
> midterm grades and decide if this is where you wish to be in your
> study of mathematics. If not, then you need to identify what
> you want to do to improve.

This was the goal-setting, identifying a difference between the real work they had been doing and the envisioned and improved quality of that work. There are few more concise definitions of problem solving than this: identify where you wish to be and where you are now. Or, define the ideal situation (the car runs smoothly) and the real situation (it won't start). The difference between the ideal and the actual is the problem that needs to be solved, the gap needing to be closed by setting a goal to do just that.

Barbara M'Gonigle had her students set a goal for the new semester: "I'm going to improve from a B to an A and here's what I'm going to do. Here's my plan." Again, this was written down in their notes. Not only did students record their objectives for themselves and for Barbara, but she asked each of them to write a letter home to their parents explaining what they intended to do.

Why write the parents? What do you think?

Yes, not only to keep them advised but also to underscore the students' responsibility to themselves and to their parents and teacher for self-development. By informing our parents we publicly acknowledge our attempts to improve to those who bear so much responsibility for our education.

Reflection and Peer Coaching

By far the most extensive program of self-improvement through goal-setting that I have ever witnessed was conducted by Hannah Magnan and Sue Steidl, two language arts teachers from a large suburban district.

Hannah's district has a well-established set of 21st century goals for its students, developed from Project 21, including critical thinking, problem solving, creativity, collaboration and communications. In addition, students are expected to demonstrate Initiative and Self-Direction by developing their own skill levels toward higher levels of mastery. Hannah and her colleagues took this goal very seriously and developed elaborate plans to enhance students' abilities to take control of their own learning.

How did she proceed with this most important process?

Setting the Stage

How do we invite students into what might be for them a territory as foreign as Spanish 1 or Introductory Biology?

Hannah had an ingenious approach, one that challenged her students to engage fully all their imaginative and contingency thinking powers:

> We play a game to get to the purpose of reflection—I have them get into teams and start with a creative visualization exercise: ("Imagine you open your eyes and find yourself in an enormous vacant lot strewn with broken glass or other miscellaneous dangers. You don't know how you got there or where you are. Lying next to you is a map with an address circled. You have a distinct feeling that at that address waits food, shelter, friends, puppies, Netflix, etc.—all the things you need to be happy. What do you do first? Why?").
>
> Each team gets a turn to tell me their chosen step. If for some reason, they can't move, they lose their turn and I go on to the next team. If they can move, they get another turn, so once they hear the ideas of others, they follow their plans and catch up immediately.

The teams generally start by saying something like "Go to the address on the map" to start. I have to say, "Great idea! You have no idea where you are. How? Lose a turn!" or they'll say "Run to a landmark you can see on the map" to which I'll reply, "You haven't taken the time to look and see, but you're barefoot."

Gradually they realize that they have to take stock of their surroundings. When they ask me to look around, I'll give them a skateboard or something as a tool; then they figure out where they are using their observations, address their immediate handicaps. They must determine how to use their tools, check their progress, review their resources, and progress in a logical fashion towards their goal. The winners get candy. We spend the rest of the discussion connecting each of these pieces to elements of the reflection and goal-setting process. (Personal communication, June, 2015)

As you can see, this imaginative game of intense visualization, and projecting into the unknown helps students take stock of where they are, what they want to do and how they might get what they want. (See Chapter Seven, "Nurturing Imaginative Behavior.")

Taking Stock of Where You Are

Just as Barbara did in college-level and advanced math, Hannah challenges students to examine their Ninth Grade writing portfolios with an eye to analyzing their strengths and weaknesses. Because her school's English department is so well-aligned, each student enters Hannah's sophomore class with a carefully revised collection of the best work from his or her freshman year. Hannah uses this work as a baseline to begin reflection and goal-setting.

In effect, they're "taking stock of where they are, their resources and challenges that they'll have to overcome to move forward." What do I like about my writing and what do I think needs improvement? This is a first-level reflection and analysis where students identify areas they believe need improvement. Notice in Figure 4.1 that students have in the past worked to improve, and gained some success. There's still room for improvement, however, in addressing our "writing obstacles." What can I do and what kinds of resources will help me? We're setting up a very logical plan for improvement.

Notice in Figure 4.1 Hannah's challenge to students to identify criteria for self-improvement: "How will I know when I have improved?" "What will I observe about my writing, about my composition processes?"

Figure 4.1

Who I was and what I did last year:

- What skill area did I work on the most on last year?

- How does this show in my work?

- What steps did I take to improve?

- What steps SHOULD I have taken that I did not?

- Was I successful in improving?

Who I am now:

- What writing strengths do I possess?

- How are they apparent in my work?

- What area is my greatest weakness? Is it the same one that I worked on last year?

- If not, what is?

- What specific examples of this weakness can I find in my writing?

Who I will be and how I will become that writer:

- What are some things I can do to address my writing obstacles?

- What resources can I leverage to continue to improve?

- How will I know when I have improved?

- How can I use reflection to help me assess my progress?

Hannah Magnan

Why ask her students to identify success criteria? Why wouldn't Hannah merely state them herself?

She's challenging them to figure out for themselves what success and accomplishment look like, just as we need to do in our own personal and professional lives.

Hannah could also add a transfer question: "In what other areas of my life might I use these kinds of reflections?" We ought to encourage students to transfer such important life-enhancing skills to other areas of their lives.

I set a goal to sail south to Antarctica when I was fourteen and without any prompting have transferred that specific process into most parts of my professional life.[2]

Establishing a Baseline/Benchmark

After Hannah has thus set the stage, she commences a literature unit, perhaps by reading Elie Wiesel's *Night*. Students are reading, analyzing, discussing

Figure 4.2   Writing Skill Breakdown

Use the list of analytical writing skill areas below to help you write your introductory reflection. For each skill area, Tier 1 is the basic skill, and Tier 2 is a more advanced application of the same skill area.

1. Skill area: Line of Inquiry

  a. Tier 1: Thesis statements and topic sentences. Clear outline and structure to paper.

  b. Tier 2: Fine tuning—considering ambiguity, alternate perspectives.

2. Skill area: Introducing and Concluding

  a. Tier 1: Proficient use of funnel format for introduction and reverse funnel for conclusion.

  b. Tier 2: Sophisticated flow to introduction, powerful, expansive conclusion.

3. Skill area: Developing an Argument

  a. Tier 1: Selecting appropriate support/evidence and citing correctly (i.e. MLA format).

  Tier 2: Choosing the relevant portion of the text support for analysis and seamlessly integrating relevant portions (thematic, not plot-based soundbytes) into argument.

  b. Tier 1: Sequencing support logically to build a powerful argument which clearly supports topic sentence and avoids repetition.

  Tier 2: Evidence is linked and goes beyond simply supporting topic sentence to showing a clear progression of pattern or idea. Argument development shows sophistication and insight. [abridged version]

Hannah Magnan and Sue Steidl

in accordance with the unit's essential questions. Then, students write a baseline or benchmark essay about this very moving work:

> *We use this work to go through the whole writing process, so I can ensure we're all speaking the same language. The end product isn't a full essay, just an essay skeleton with a complete intro/conclusion and one full fleshed out body paragraph. I give a ton of feedback on this during each step of the process, using the same goal-setting language when referencing their skill development. I've found that the thought "It gives us a common language" goes a long way when they are reflecting.*

Then, Hannah encourages students to select an area for improvement (see Figure 4.2).

In Figure 4.2 we can see the different levels of complexity in Tiers 1 and 2. A basic thesis statement provides structure, but students who want to achieve greater mastery must understand complexity, ambiguity and different perspectives as is appropriate for arguing about multi-faceted issues like food stamps, health care, and conflicts found within history and literature.

Notice also the importance of "developing an argument." This means that presenting a thesis statement is setting forth a claim, giving good reasons with supportive, relevant and verifiable evidence. We shall see how Andy Snyder works with these aspects of argument in social studies in Chapter Ten.

Figure 4.3 Making an Argument

Making an argument involves analyzing a complex situation or phenomenon and stating a claim or a thesis statement. Each such statement will be:

Concise and Complex
Arguable/Analytical
Provable
and Specific

Thus, we see that a thesis statement presents an argument about a complex issue or phenomenon, one that must be proved with specific details and evidence. The thesis statement in language arts is as similar to a claim about relationships within physics and biology, for example, as it is between cause and effect in history.

Hannah Magnan

Peer Feedback

Now, here's the step that surprised me. Students weren't working on their goals alone. No, they were to be with their classmates every step of the way. Each student would be responsible for providing her classmates with extensive feedback about the goals toward which they were working. In other words, peers were as responsible for helping their classmates as for reaching their own goals.

As I said above, virtually every self-help book I've ever read focuses upon your attaining your own goals, by persistently, daily reminding yourself, even visualizing having already attained success with this goal. Writing them down, of course, is paramount as well.

What Hannah is doing, rather, is to emphasize that few of us work toward our goals in isolation, and that vital to our success is our ability to form mutually beneficial, interdependent partnerships with our peers. I once read an article about a very famous automobile manufacturer (Japanese) whose executives had to post their annual objectives for all to see. Perhaps making them public meant not only that everybody acknowledged his or her intentions, but also that each department could help the others as they should. Working and learning together toward common ends is the hallmark of success in today's personal and professional worlds.[3]

Once students have an idea about the nature and purpose of feedback, then they are ready to select a goal and Hannah forms Goal Groups. The ones I was most aware of focused upon students developing their abilities to write improved, deeper and more meaningful thesis statements and conclusions. (See Figure 4.3.)

This may seem easy to the lay person, but if you think about what goes into making an argument about a complex social or scientific issue, you realize that there's a lot of analysis that must precede the crafting of a thesis. In fact, it might be one of the last things a writer does—craft the opening sentence.

Hannah used direct teaching about thesis statements. They should meet these criteria: CAPS, meaning Concise/Complex; Arguable/Analytical; Provable using whole text; and Specific. She would give students models such as the following to critique: "Juliet needed more freedom . . ." "In addition to love, a primary theme in *Romeo and Juliet* is the danger of holding a grudge." And then models of better thesis statements: "By empathizing with the struggle some individuals face to feel free, Scout is able to surpass her initial misjudgments of others and recognize that each person deserves respect," and "Since Holden lacks self-confidence and is dissatisfied with who he is as an individual, he is unable to form meaningful relationships with other adults" (Magnan, Personal communications, June, 2015).

Here's Hannah's explanation of what follows Goal-Setting Group Formation:

> *Students research skill deficits individually, and then are assigned to a group with similar difficulties. Together they make a list of their common problem areas centered around their selected goal, review all sources and create an annotated bibliography with the writing center and their four best additional sources. These sources are selected based on their usefulness to the project, and are evaluated and summarized in their annotations.*
>
> *Great Goal Action Plan—Next, based on their common issues and research into how to combat them, students create proposals for how they will achieve their goals including examining models, practicing skills, etc. Teacher approval is required for: a.) group statement of problem, b.) plan of action, c.) method of assessment (i.e. how they will know they have learned the skill—this cannot be linked to a grade, but must be something they identify about their own writing). Each step must be approved before moving on to the next step. When all three steps are approved the proposal is complete.*

Notice that students don't make an action plan until they've done some background research on good writing, specifically how to write a good topic sentence. And, there's included an answer to the question, "How do we know when we've improved, begun to reach our goals?" "What's the evidence of our success?"

Planning, Monitoring and Evaluating

A goal-setting framework similar to what Barbara and Hannah have engaged in lends itself to a simple three-step process, one as applicable to developing the depth of one's thinking as to setting sail for Antarctica by the time you're fifty.

Here are three sets of questions that can serve as an organizing overlay for this process:

Planning: What's my goal? What specifically do I wish to achieve? How will I achieve it? What's my plan?

Monitoring: How well am I doing? What progress am I making? Do I need to modify the goal?

Evaluating: At the end of the process, how well did I do? What worked well? What do I need to improve upon and why?

This triumvirate of questions is what empowers each of us toward more fulfilling accomplishments. Here we take control of our learning and our lives.[4]

It's interesting to me that Hannah has students work collaboratively on a "group statement of the problem." It is in this statement that we need to define clearly the difference between the ideal and the realities of our own writing. And, as we know from good problem solving, an accurate statement of the problem is key to finding one or more acceptable solutions.

Group Writing, Feedback and Video Creation

Henceforth, we're on to new units, perhaps now reading and acting out *Macbeth* (see Chapter Seven, "Nurturing Imaginative Thinking"), more writing, group peer feedback and while waiting for teacher feedback at one point students are busy translating what they've been learning into a different medium: from the written word to a video episode. These were a lot of fun to make, judging from the ones I saw where students in the same Goal Group were advertising the significance of this aspect of their writings and, perhaps, how to go about improving them with tips for improvement.

Students avoid a situation of what Hannah called "the blind leading the blind," because she has created two feedback groups. One is where they work for their specific goals; the second is where they can leverage their strengths for the benefit of others. If one is good at structure, but weak in argument, for example, she can offer her strengths while benefitting from the insights of others. "This," says Hannah, "is a skill I really want them to take into the 'real world.'"

Having challenged students to dramatize concepts such as "misogynist" and "egoist" in high school, and great dramas like *Crime and Punishment* in college, I can attest to the efficacy of having to think about a concept like "guilt" or "democracy" in visual and dramatic rather than only in linguistic modes.

Following critiques of the group videos, there's more peer and teacher feedback until we get to drafting a final essay.

Second Semester Revisions

During the second iteration of this process, in the Spring, Hannah made some important modifications to this process:

1. *Discussion about helpful and unhelpful feedback, and how students are responsible for filtering for good advice.*

Not all feedback is helpful and we need to zero in on that which works well and why.

2. *In homogeneous goal groups, students develop lists of common difficulties and research potential solutions using the writing center as their primary resource, focusing on provided models and feedback.*

Another aspect of the reflection process, monitoring progress: What works and what does not?

For example, to be effective feedback should be direct (to the person), immediate (not the day after tomorrow), specific (related to detailed items in one's writing), suggest or lead to options for improvement. Feedback is least helpful when it is ambiguous, non-specific ("You've got issues with structure"), long-delayed, emotionally laden ("Umm, that makes no sense").

3. *During composition, students first meet in goal groups to implement initial stages of their plan of action. As they write, with each collected composition step, students included a brief description of how they pursued their goal during this step.*

Here we're focusing on how they proceeded and why. These reflections might be the most important of all, for here is where we learn what has worked and why. Without such reflections our strivings are less significant because we do not know to account for our successes or failures:

My group helped with the thesis statements, something I've had a lot of trouble with in the past . . .

With plenty of support I figured out how to get better at providing good evidence.

Seems as if I've always, and maybe always will, have problems organizing my stuff, my argument . . . "What goes where?" isn't easy for me at all!

4. *Students revise essay using teacher and peer feedback. With paper submission, students complete their final goal reflection using a prompt and are assessed using the reflection rubric.*

Figure 4.4 Reflection Rubric

So far this year, we have done a lot of goal-setting and skill practice. You have evaluated your own work and accessed your feedback to determine your biggest writing obstacles, then worked collaboratively to brainstorm and implement plans to address your difficulties. Now it's time to reflect on your journey. Reflect on your progress towards your writing goal, and how your pursuit has affected your learning.

1. What was your specific goal?
2. Do you think you picked the right goal?
3. Could you have used more guidance choosing your goal?
4. What have you done to improve in your goal area? What specific steps of your proposal have you pursued?
5. Have you seen results? What?
6. How did the process of Goal-Setting help you?
7. Where do you feel like you needed more instruction?
8. Did you see evidence of improvement in your essay as a result of the process?
9. What role did reflection play in your growth?
10. What was the most important aspect of this experience?
11. What did you learn about yourself?
12. How might these lessons learned be transferred to other areas of life?

Hannah Magnan

Let me emphasize one question in Figure 4.4, the reflection rubric: "What role did reflection play in your growth?" Students would vary in their crediting this not-too-often-taught process of self-reflection: Hannah recalls students noting that when they analyzed their papers they weren't sure why something was good or not. They couldn't tell her why they couldn't "close read a text," for example. Having to put into words what they "didn't know" was the most difficult part of the reflection–self-development process.

This is the basic outline of how Hannah has proceeded over two years with different language arts classes.

As you can see, this is not merely setting a goal and striving for it. No, it involves the intense process of doing so and monitoring your progress all along the way. The navigator sets a course for her ship, toward a destination. But she knows that winds, currents and weather will set her off course. Therefore, we take sightings, in my day of the Sun and stars, to take an accurate measure of exactly where we are and how we need to adjust our courses to arrive at our final destination.

Conclusion

Recently, a survey found that half of college graduates studied "lacked clear goals or a sense of direction two years after graduation" (Arum & Roksa, 2014).

The process we've described in this chapter may seem easy, but I'm sure the students in Barbara's and Hannah's classes would tell us that it took a lot of time, hard work and that they probably wouldn't have striven to improve their work without their constant, attentive and loving pressure to do so.

Again, why is Barbara's, Hannah's and Sue's work here so important?

What they have done is to set their students on a journey with a clear mindset: "If I want to get somewhere, I will need to identify clearly where I wish to be and how to get there. Most of this is within my own control, at least to ask myself, 'Where do I wish to go in life?'" We'll learn the importance of collaborating with friends and colleagues along the way.

Hannah's very structured approach may just help students think more productively when they're out on the highways and byways of life, out on their own where they must think for themselves. What she has provided them is a thinking frame, a reflective approach that will become deeply embedded within their encounters with difficult life situations: going to college, becoming a professional person who has a guiding philosophy.

"If I wish to get somewhere in school and in life, I must make choices. These choices are within my control to make, monitor and evaluate."[5] It's not luck, fate nor, in most cases, somebody else who will control my living a rewarding life. It's up to me to take the wheel of my own ship, set a destination, a course and continually modify my approach toward those new territories.

Application

1. Under what circumstances have you set specific goals for your own success and/or improvement? How well did you succeed? What did you learn from the process? What to stress and what, if anything, to avoid?

2. When have you challenged your students to set goals for their own improvement? How well did this work? What do you think your students learned from the process?

3. Which intellectual skills at the heart of your subject are appropriate for students to practice goal-setting?

4. In planning a unit of instruction, or the commencement of a new year of teaching your subject, how might you go about challenging students to set goals?

   a. What would serve as their benchmark? A previous year's portfolio? A mid-term or final exam? A final exhibition or capstone project?

   b. How would you encourage students to monitor their progress and when? How can you leverage peer group support as Hannah did?

   c. What kinds of feedback could you give them?

   d. How would your students assess their final outcomes? Their achievement of goals?

   e. How might students relate this reflective experience to other areas of their lives?

Notes

1. I have written extensively about this adventure in *Quest for Antarctica—A Journey of Wonder and Discovery* (2007).

2. It may have been the polar explorers' modeling goal-setting for me, but it could easily have been my father's constantly challenging me with his maxims: "Make your plan and work your plan." This message driven home during my high school years was always accompanied by his Churchillian command, "There's no such word as 'CAN'T.' It should be banished from the English language."

3. See General Stanley McChrystal's recent book, *Team of Teams* (2015).

4. See Barbara McCombs' work on metacognition, "Metacognition and motivation for higher level thinking" (1991). See also Carol Dweck *Mindset* (2007).

5. See Carol Dweck *Mindset* (2007) and Marilee Adams *Change Your Questions, Change Your Life* (2009). These excellent resources focus upon the power each of us possesses to change the course of her life by adapting a growth-oriented mindset and by asking ourselves different questions: "What do I want for myself and others?"

References

Adams, M. (2009) *Change Your Questions, Change Your Life.* San Francisco: Berrett-Koehler.

Arum, R., & Roksa, J. (2014) *Aspiring Adults Adrift.* Chicago: University of Chicago Press. Quoted by David Brooks (2015), "How Adulthood Happens," 12 June, *The New York Times*, p. A27.

Dweck, C.S. (2007) *Mindset—The new psychology of success, how we can learn to fulfill our potential*. New York: Ballantine Books.

McChrystal, S. (2015) *Team of Teams—New rules of engagement for a complex world*. New York: Portfolio.

McCombs, B. (1991) "Metacognition and motivation for higher level thinking." Paper presented at the annual meeting of the American Educational Research Association, Chicago.

Chapter 5

Enhancing Inquiry

The Essence of Life

"Teaching Happens When . . ."

A language arts teacher recently asked me, "Why do we want students to ask better questions in class, anyway?"

A fair question! Why bother attempting to observe, monitor and learn from the kinds of questions students do and do not ask? Why would it, for that matter, be important for us to learn about our own inquiry processes?

I always urge educators to become very good observers of the kinds of questions we ask and those we tend to shy away from. Why? So we can share how our minds work with our students. To serve as good models. To communicate that we are always inquiring, even if we do not enunciate specific questions about that which puzzles, intrigues, surprises and baffles us.

We want to know how well our students inquire, because we believe that there's more to life than asking "Jeopardy" kinds of factual recall questions. Sure, that information can win you a lot of money and we need factual information in order to reason. And that's the clincher, we need to know how to reason through the very difficult situations in life and ferreting out the causes, reasons and best approaches to these problematic experiences (e.g. health care, global warming, the economy, our future) will not result from merely asking "Yes/No," one-word-answer kinds of questions.

We will not be able to survive intelligently in our new world by always being asked multiple-choice, fill-in-the-bubble kinds of questions. This is how one foreign exchange student from Germany characterized learning in her host school here in the United States: as doing multiple-choice questions where you don't have to think. (See Chapter Thirteen, "Rude Awakening for Professional Development.")

But there's another reason that goes to the heart of this book and to the very essence of education.

. . . teaching happens when a person begins learning (on his own) how to do certain things. *It happens when that person freely chooses to extend himself in order to find answers to questions he poses for himself, when he acts to move beyond what he has learned by rote . . .* [It] happens when a student begins to understand what he is doing, when he becomes capable of giving reasons and seeing connections within his experiences, when he recognizes the errors he or someone else is making and can propose what should be done to set things right. (Emphasis added, Greene, 1973)

In other words, inquiry, when freely engaged in, is a mark of what good teaching develops within all of us, the desire to expand our horizons and adventure into these new domains.

Approach—Social Studies and Language Arts

As with our other chapters my attempt here is to present ways of observing and then drawing conclusions about students' inquiries using various models and frameworks. We should be able to generalize from the experiences of Stephen Lazar in social studies and Beth Krone, language arts, to our own special subjects and/or grade level challenges.

Observing Questions

As with other educators mentioned in this book, we have given students various kinds of pre and post assessments, or benchmarks. In the cases of Steve and Beth, the benchmarks were administered early in their one semester (January to June) courses. In both cases students were challenged to pose meaningful questions about an historical event (the US forces in Afghanistan) and an American play *(Our Town)*. The post assessment gathered information from their questions about different events—current events in Ukraine and from *Twelfth Night.*

In history, students were pursuing answers to their original questions as historians would logically do to achieve a depth of understanding.

In language arts questioning assumed a role different from that of conducting research. As students read *Our Town, A Raisin in the Sun* and *Twelfth Night* Beth engaged them in analyzing text, becoming aware of various lenses that would help them understand plot, character, symbolism and themes: Feminism, Marxism, Critical Theory. She also conducted weekly "Socratic

Seminars" on different segments of each play. During these fish-bowl-type discussions (inner circle discusses—outer circle analyzes action), she would often ask, "What words/phrases in this act spark your interest? What are you wondering about?" Students in the outer circle were charged with keeping track of and reporting on, for example, the number of students who posed questions, responded to each other, participated and the like.

In neither class was there anything resembling a direct teaching of different levels of questions as we've seen before (Barell, 2007). Students were actively engaged in thinking critically about historical and literary issues, problems of interpretation and the like.

Below you will see quite different results from both classes. In the one class, Steve's, you will see significant growth and change over time in the kind and quality of students' questions. In Beth's class we have different, yet significant results in our focus on students' inquiry.

Frameworks for Analysis

One of the most intriguing and exciting aspects of conducting direct, observational data-gathering research like this is the opportunity to read and analyze students' work. As a former English teacher here in New York City, I, like millions of other teachers, have spent years doing just this—that is, analyzing students' work. We've been searching for their understanding of major concepts—from relationships between weight and mass in science to the nature of a tragic hero, for example.

With the samples below we're looking for how students' posing inquiries about complex, ambiguous, puzzling situations might have developed over time.

To do this we use a number of different frameworks:

Torrance Test of Creativity

This test (www.ststesting.com/ngifted.html, accessed August, 2015) uses these concepts with which to analyze and discuss students' responses to several different creative thinking challenges ("How many uses can you find for a used tire?" and "What if all the ice in Antarctica melted?"; the latter is my own question similar to Torrance's):

Fluency: How many responses did the student write down?

Flexibility: What different points of view did the students' responses reflect?[1]

Originality: How were students' answers different from others'?

Elaboration: The amount of detail in the response?

Figure 5.1   Three Story Intellect

Level III: Applying/Using Knowledge to Demonstrate Understanding

> Evaluate
> Judge
> Imagine
> Speculate . . . if . . . then
> Estimate
> Apply a principle
> Forecast
> Create a product

Level II: Processing Information (in order to understand)

> Compare/contrast
> Classify
> Identify variables
> Analyze
> Distinguish cause and effect/fact and opinion
> Pose problems, generate solutions and solve
> Make decisions
> Infer and draw conclusions
> Hypothesize, experiment and draw conclusions
> Explain (why), justify decisions/conclusions

Level I: Gathering Information

> Describe   Name
> Observe   Recite
> Record Data   Recall

Source: Fogarty, Robin J. Problem-Based Learning & Other Curriculum Models for the Multiple Intelligences Classroom. Copyright © 1997 by Corwin Press. Reprinted by permission of SAGE Publications, Inc.

This framework gives us several ways of analyzing questions. Which ones do you think would be most reflective of growth in thinking/inquiring?

The Three Story Intellect (Figure 5.1)

Notice here we have a three-tiered framework to reflect on: Level I—Gathering Information; Level II—Processing Information; and Level III—Applying What We've Learned.

A major function of this framework is to alert us to the different cognitive levels of questions the students are writing. For example, in analyzing Beth's pre-assessment from *Our Town*, I found that most of the questions asked for motivation, "Why did Emily want to return to her 12th birthday?" or about Thornton Wilder's writing, "Why did TW give stage directions only to the dead people?"

However, there were two students who posed Level III questions, asking "What if?" this had occurred ("If Emily had returned to the past, what would happen? Would it change?") Not many Level IIIs, however.

This is a most valuable tool, especially when we notice that students are posing mainly Level I questions: "Where is Afghanistan?" "Who is Malvolio?" and "What did Walter do with the $10,000?" If we made such an observation, what would we do about it?

How could we encourage and help students pose more in-depth Level II and Level III questions? From Sixth Grade (Kerry Faber in Edmonton, Barell, 2007) to Ann Marie Di Lorenzo in college biology I've seen teachers use this framework (posted in the room) as a guide to identify those questions that make greater cognitive demands on all of us—the "Why?" "How do we solve?" kinds of question.

Beyond mere identification, we can use the more challenging questions as models, share them with students, post them around the room, perhaps. We can, obviously, practice all these questions so that students become good at asking "What if?" and "Why not?" questions. The goal, of course, is to help them pose these on their own, spontaneously, as part of their genuine search for good solutions or to acquire deeper understandings. So we highlight them, discuss them, play out the possibilities. In responding to such "What if?" questions in history or in literature our responses must, of course, be grounded in the logic of characters' behavior, beliefs and responses to other events. It's not "anything goes."

I've often used this as an excellent model for learning, a kind of information processing model:

Intake—Information, Data, Facts.

Process—Think about it: analyze, solve problems, critique and explain findings.

Apply—Use information to go beyond the problem/issue: "What if?" Speculate/project findings into novel situations (resembles Bloom's eponymous level).

International Baccalaureate

The International Baccalaureate (ibo.org) has a framework that helps teachers guide students' inquiries about subjects. It consists of these concepts:

Form

Function

Connection

Causality

Change

Perspective

Responsibility

Reflection.

You can see how such concepts can help us analyze the kinds of questions we do and do not ask. (See Barell, 2012 for how these were used in a Vancouver kindergarten class to demonstrate students' growth.)

Concepts We Create from Our Analyses

One of Steve's students, Vanessa, asks about the Israeli–Palestinian conflict, "What does each side believe is the root of the conflict?"

Yes, this calls for Level II, Causal Explanation, but the word "believe" might introduce considerations of beliefs, religious, historical, personal and the like. We might be entering what Benjamin Bloom called the realm of Affect and we know that one of his taxonomies focused entirely upon that dimension.

These are just some ways of analyzing students' questions. You will generate others. The important consideration is to examine students' work very closely and attempt to come to some understanding of what they are telling us through their inquiries.

Doing History Backwards

Normally, we teach history from, say, the founding of the country forward to the Civil War and thence up as far as we can make it into the twentieth century. But historians are always asking "What?" and "Why?" and "With what effects?" about various events, for example, World War II.

Stephen Lazar took a different approach. Starting with the war in Afghanistan, he introduced his students to a model and contemporary conflict. Students analyzed a specific situation involving US troops and then he presented his first benchmark, "What do you wish to know about this conflict?" Another way of phrasing this might have been, "As a professional historian (or journalist) what do you need to find out about this conflict?"

From here students moved to the Crimean struggle (2014, resulting in Russian annexation) and after similar study, students posed more questions and sought out causes of that situation tracing its history back beyond World War II to the Russian Revolution of 1917. Finally, each selected another world conflict and, as a final benchmark, posed questions for investigation and reflection about that.

The Results

Here are Cora's February questions:

1. Why is Muhammad thankful for the armed US drone attacks?
2. What does "When the US leaves the Taliban will get red eyes" mean?
3. After the villagers saved the soldier, will their life be harder because of the Taliban's threats?

And then here are Jerry's:

1. What caused the Taliban's hatred to the US?
2. How can the problem be solved?
3. We're [sic] there similar events in the world?

 Reflective Pause

What similarities and differences do you see between these students' questions? What kinds of questions (Bloom/Three Story Intellect) are used?

First, we notice that both students are justly interested in finding root causes of the situations they have been studying.

Second, you will notice how Jerry is more focused upon problem identification and resolution. This might reflect a stronger sense of the need to probe deeply into the root causes of the problem.

Third, you will note that Jerry asks about "similar events in the world." This calls for the very complex analysis of comparison and contrast, a process we know from Marzano et al.'s research (2001) that directly and positively affects achievement/learning.

But, let us not dismiss Cora's thoughts prematurely. Note how she asks a very complex question calling for evaluation (formerly the highest of Bloom's taxonomy): Will the villagers' lives "be harder"?

What does this call for? Yes, making a prediction, but one that to be logical must be based upon clear citations of good reasons and evidence. We can make reasonable predictive conclusions if they are based on thorough knowledge of facts on the ground, philosophies, past history and, perhaps, analogizing with similar situations.

So, as with the essential question Steve asks for this unit, "What makes it complicated?" We see complexity in these students' questions. Both are asking about causation. One calls for making predictions and the other is interested in that equally important historical intellectual process, making comparisons, similar to analogical reasoning and creation of metaphors.

And, as we know, not everybody would agree upon direct and indirect causes for any conflict. I submit historians have differed over causes of the American Revolution, for example, as well as the Civil War.

We also need to compare and contrast each student's before-and-after questions.

So, here are Cora's final benchmark questions about the conflict in Syria:

1. Why did the Syrian forces starve the civilians?

2. Why did the Syrian forces use starvation as a weapon? How is it used as a weapon?

3. How did the Syrian Starvation happen?

And, here are Jerry's about the conflict between North and South Korea:

1. What is the main issue between North and South Korea?

2. What are differences between North and South Koreans?

3. What are the relations between North Korea with other countries and South Korea with other countries?

 ## Reflective Pause

Again, what similarities and differences do you see?
How do you think each student's historical thinking has changed? Has it?

Moving from What to *What If?*

With Cora we see more in-depth interest in causality. All three questions ask for possible, reasonable causes. No questions about meanings, although these could involve deep analysis as well.

With Jerry, when we read his explanations we see his strong concern for "differences," for "different views." More comparison and contrast, especially implied with his third question about relationships amongst North/South Korea and other nations. This goes beyond what *might* be perceived as a simplistic "What's the problem?" and "How can we solve it?" to taking a more in-depth look at foreign relationships amongst all countries having dealings with North/South Korea. But, on the other hand, his concern might yield primarily descriptive data: this is the situation without calling for much analysis. It all depends on what he's doing with the data—describing and/or analyzing. Maybe he's repeating what he heard in class?

We need to be reminded that the logical step following any comparison and contrast—be it between North and South Korea or between Lady Macbeth and Agrippina—is to use the comparisons and contrasts in order to draw logical conclusions about these people. We don't just create a Venn diagram and leave it at that. We ask, "So, what do we learn from these analogies and comparisons?"

Now, let's take a look at two other students in Steve's class, Wilette and Vanessa. Here are the initial questions Wilette posed about the US involvement with Afghanistan:

1. When is the US going to leave Afghanistan?
2. Why didn't the US complete any of the promises they made to the village?
3. Why was this important to make it into a movie?

After several months' study that involved doing extensive research on elements involved in the Crimean controversy with Russia and Ukraine, Wilette posed these questions about civil strife in South Sudan:

1. How did the situation start?
2. Who is involved? (Are there certain parties or groups of people, maybe political leaders?)
3. Is there any good that can come out of their situation?

Notice here Wilette's continuing concern for causation, "How did the situation start?" "Who is involved?" And, I assume, "Why are they fighting?"

But notice also her last question: "Is there any good that can come out of their situation?" In her lengthy explanation, Wilette phrases her puzzlement this way:

> The reason why I chose the third question is because the whole point of this class is to realize that history is complicated and to find out why they are complicated. So I posed this question because the violence in south Sudan may look like it's all bad, but *what if it is doing some good?* That question will help me find out how the situation is complicated. (Emphasis added)

Wilette's last question is a good example of contingency thinking, asking the "What if?" question. We ask it all the time in science (Einstein's "What if I rode along a ray of light, what would I observe?") and sometimes in history, although some historians avoid this kind of "What if?" question as unrealistic, or un-historical. (See Chapter Three, "Developing Abstract Reasoning" and The Peel Test of Contingency Thinking.)

But notice how she demands that we take a different point of view, a different perspective on the situation. She challenges us to look at the terrible conflict to see if something "good" might grow out of tragedy. Maybe she's optimistic; maybe she wants us to confront the real possibility that people can come together, settle differences and build a better society.

This contingency thinking is an element of what Piaget called Formal Operational Thought, a transition from reasoning from concrete objects/experiences, to the ability to reason about abstractions, hold two or more of these in one's mind simultaneously, project consequences into the near and far future.

Wilette's question can also be seen as an imaginative one (Chapter Four), because she is shifting our focus from bad to potentially good. She's re-orienting our thinking toward considering alternative possibilities, questioning thereby the common wisdoms of conventional thought.

Not all students attain this ability—and, neither do all adults. And not in all subjects. Wilette is showing a propensity here in history, and she might in literature, but not in math, for example.

If we think contingency, more abstract reasoning is important for the education of an adolescent, we might highlight these kinds of questions, provide students with opportunities to respond to the same as well as raise their own. With practice and understanding, comes meaningfulness.

And, finally, what do we see in comparing Vanessa's February questions with her May questions? First, in February, about Afghanistan:

1. Why did Gulab decide to help, knowing the consequences? [Causation]

2. What were the intentions of the soldier being there? [Describe/Analyze?]

3. How does the relationship between Afghanistan and United States change after this incident? [Describe what happened? Predict?]

And in May about the Israeli–Palestinian conflict:

1. What started the [Israeli–Palestinian] conflict? [Causation]

2. How does nationalism [play] a role in the conflict between these two nations? [Explain role of nationalism]

3. What does each side believe is the root of the conflict? [Explain two different points of view]

What changes in historical, analytic thinking do you see here?

Note the introduction of the concept "nationalism," and the role it plays in the conflict. Invoking this concept will call for a far more in-depth analysis than what she called for in February.

Note also a question none of the other students posed: "What does each side believe?" This is a perspective-taking kind of question, one that should also become more prevalent during adolescence, as Formal Operations mature.

In asking questions about differing points of view, we are challenging others and ourselves to think like another person, to put ourselves in somebody else's situation, to see the world as he sees it. Not always easy, especially if we attempt to be empathic. This, like the comparison/contrast question, requires a good deal of background knowledge.

How do we use "What if?" questions in science and math?

What if we alter any of the variables in this problem? How would that change the outcomes?

What if we observe this kind of result, what are the possible ways of manipulating variables to achieve it?

In order to help students with these kinds of questions we will have to model this for them. As we will see in Mike's Physics 1 class, Chapter Eleven, this can be done with any system like a swinging pendulum: "What do you see?" "What are the elements/aspects/variables we can alter?" You will see how he uses this systems analysis to lead to testable questions: "If we lengthen the string, reduce size/weight of pendulum, what do you predict will happen?" We can do the same in literature: "Here's a play with these elements/characters. What if we change one or two?" Same for math: "What if we alter one or more of these variables/quantities in this problem?"

But again, we'll have to model this kind of behavior perhaps many times to help students then analyze a fresh system for its own elements and variables.

And how do we vary points of view?

> Suppose you were any one of these different professionals
> analyzing this complex issue (crime statistics, health care data . . .):
> mathematician, social worker, biologist/nutritionist/medical
> doctor . . . How might your analysis and perspective vary and why?

A Growth in Complexity

Thus, in both Wilette's and Vanessa's questions we see by semester's end a growth in complexity of their analytical thinking:

"What if?" contingency thinking—requiring really in-depth knowledge of the situation, of involved parties, their motives, methods and materials; perhaps comparisons with other similar civil strife situations—perhaps the American Civil War? That in Vietnam?

In Vanessa's case, explaining the role of a driving force in world history, "nationalism." And, the very complex task of taking another's point of view and reasoning therefrom. We can see this as the essence of making Counter Claims with Good Reasons and Evidence. (See Chapter Nine, "Playgrounds of the Mind.")

We see neither kinds of analysis in Cora's or Jerry's thinking, before and after. In Cora's and Jerry's cases, we see very strong emphasis on causation, a primary inquiry within all of historical studies.

Wilette and Vanessa have added significantly to their own thinking about history and to ours. Without these kinds of questions—the conceptual and "What if?"—we might get stuck in merely listing the kinds of causes scholars have identified for these conflicts in their on-line editorials, Wikipedia articles and the like.

The answers to "What if?" questions, too seldom asked, will not be found in Wikipedia. Hence, they call for more original analyses.

Explaining the role of an abstract and so transferrable concept like "nationalism" will, of course, have many more citations, but using this concept to analyze a current situation might also call for more original thinking.

Beth's Playwriting Class

When Beth told me she wanted to take a look at students' questioning, we developed a set of benchmark opportunities within two of the three plays she was teaching, Thornton Wilder's *Our Town*, the first play, and the last one, *Twelfth Night*.

Our expectation, at least mine, was that we would see growth over time in the fluency—the total number—of students' questions from first to last.

We did not.

Why might this be the case with directions that asked students to write (as per Torrance's measures) as many and as different kinds of questions about this episode as you can? Some students wrote six questions about *Our Town* in March and four about Shakespeare in June. Others had an even more dramatic reduction!

Why?

It occurs to me that several factors might be at play:

1. The difference between Wilder and Shakespeare, in terms of plot, language, character and the like.

2. Time of year. The final benchmark was given during the semester's penultimate week. Not a good time, maybe!

3. Students' interest in either play itself.

4. How directions might have been given (I did not witness the same).

5. Other reasons?

Let us look at another Torrance criterion, Flexibility, or point of view or scope.

Oliver, a very engaged student who always participated fully in the Socratic Seminars, from Wilder through Shakespeare, wrote five analytic Level II questions about *Our Town*, e.g.: "Why does Wilder give stage directions to the dead people and not the live ones?" "Does Wilder have a specific idea of how dead people act?" And three about the funeral, e.g.—"Whose is it?" "Does the suspense hurt or help the play?"

Good questions about the playwright's craft.

He wrote two questions about Shakespeare: "What is the main motivation in the book?" and "How does the time period affect the writing?"

What do we notice about the focus of his questions in the second round?

He has broadened his scope from being curious about the playwright's craft to 1. a focus upon what Aristotle would call the "action," the driving purpose,[2] of the play and 2. how Elizabethan culture might have affected Shakespeare's writing.

Fewer questions, yes, but different ones and equally valuable, from a different perspective (International Bachalaureate criteria, point of view; Torrance, Flexibility).

Another student, Jailene, did ask more questions in June than in March. And one of her questions follows this pattern of coming at the play from a different point of view: "What does the title *Twelfth Night* mean?"

This not only introduces a different point of view (Flexibility), but it is also original with this class. No other students had posed this kind of question either in March nor June.

Kevin asked the same number of questions about Wilder and Shakespeare, but there's a difference:

March: "Why was the play told like this?"

June: "What is the main theme established in the play?" "Does this play connect to the other plays William Shakespeare has written?"

What differences do you see?

As you note, some students grew from a focus primarily on the art and craft of Wilder to an interest in issues of the broader society and connections amongst Shakespeare's other plays.

David was another student whose initial questions focused singularly upon Emily and other characters' actions, but he also asked this: "Was it Wilder's intention to make the dead world another community?" and "Was it thought that a woman's job was to bring a baby into the world?" Notice the focus on society beyond the play here.

He was also puzzled by his observation that only the King and fool "tell the truth (and don't sneak around) [why?] because that's how he felt society was in that time?"

And one student, Michelle, asked about *Twelfth Night*: "Could this be a text that led to the expanding of same sex love?" "Were people ever against this text?"

These students are thinking beyond the text to wonder about issues within Elizabethan society. The scope of their questions has been enlarged, perhaps because the notion of same sex relationships is so much a part of our 21st century world.

Several students found *Our Town* boring and unrelated to their own lives.

One such was Sarah who about *Twelfth Night* reprised this question with: "How do these events affect my life?"

So, in the end we have reasons why students might not have posed more questions about Shakespeare, but a number of them broadened the dimensions of their inquiries to explore other territories, other facets of life behind the play itself.

Conclusion

Observing and monitoring students' inquisitiveness, their curiosities, their puzzlements and questions throughout a semester or year-long course can be most rewarding when we see these kinds of changes over time.

Asking different, more complex questions can lead to deeper understanding of the situations we are examining.

Learning from others' questions is something that always occurs when we work in groups where we are challenged to observe, reflect and question, be we groups of adults or of our students.

To begin to pose these kinds of questions, spontaneously, on our own, is one significant goal of teaching and education as Maxine Greene (1973) has asserted.

Application

1. What kinds of questions do students pose in your classes?

2. How might you gather information about the kinds of questions they ask:

   a. Inquiry journals. I used these in literature throughout my career as a college teacher of world literature. They can be handwritten on paper as well as done electronically. Students can keep journals weekly recording their major inquiries, findings and reflective thoughts about same, thus engaging in the cycle of inquiry.

   b. Use before-and-after benchmark assessments as Stephen and Beth did.

   c. Periodically have students read, review and reflect on their own inquiry processes: "What do I notice about my questions? What kinds are they? How have they changed since the beginning of this journal?"

3. In a unit you are planning, how might you gather before and after data?

4. In a unit you are teaching or will teach, how can you give students opportunities to ask "What if?" questions modeled after the ones we ask?

5. Given a story, historical event, complex social problem with numbers, what elements might we vary to achieve different outcomes? How can we encourage students to analyze such situations with the taking of different points of view in mind?

6. Have students find examples of the good questions they encounter in their own readings, in and out of school, or heard in general media. For example, as of this writing a significant agreement has been negotiated

with a major international power. The advocates are justly asking, "If you do not like this agreement, what is a viable alternative?" and critics are asking, "How can you trust them to carry out their end of the deal?" The search for alternatives and for evidence of trust are important questions to ask here.

Notes

1. You will note that this classification has been changed to "Resistance to premature closure." I choose to remain with the prior category—Flexibility—because of its power to analyze inquiry. And because researcher David Perkins, Harvard Project Zero, claims that Flexibility of thinking is more a criterion for Creativity than is Fluency, the number of responses. Stands to reason.

2. See Francis Fergusson (1949), *The Idea of a Theater*, pp. 242–244.

References

Barell, J. (2007) *Why Are School Buses Always Yellow? Teaching inquiry pre-K to 5.* Thousand Oaks, CA: Corwin Press.

Barell, J. (2012) *How Do We Know They're Getting Better? Assessment for 21st century capacities, K–8.* Thousand Oaks, CA: Corwin Press.

Fergusson, F. (1949) *The Idea of a Theater.* Princeton NJ: Princeton University Press.

Greene, M. (1973) *Teacher as Stranger.* Belmont, CA: Wadsworth.

Marzano, R., Pickering, D., & Pollock, J. (2001) *Classroom Instruction That Works— Research-based strategy for increasing segued achievement.* Alexandria, VA: Association for Supervision and Curriculum Development.

Chapter 6

Modeling

How We All Learn

What became apparent in various observed classes during this three-year project is that teachers proceeded by creating what I'm going to call "model experiences," ones that presented learning challenges within a framework that was duplicated time and time again.

For example, during the first week, Mike Zitolo in physics laid out on top of his huge black science lab table a simple pendulum in front of students sitting at seven smaller traditional lab tables. He set it in motion and asked students first to "Describe this system." In using this word-system Mike introduced them to a familiar concept, but now they were going to do something different, that is, break it down into its component parts. (In human biology we speak of the digestive, circulatory and respiratory systems; in civics, of transportation and water systems; and in climatology, of weather systems.)

Students thought individually, wrote notes, conferred and then shared observations in the best Think, Pair and Share protocol:

S: I see gravity.

T: Gravity plays a role. Do you see it or infer it?

S: Infer.

T: How do you define a "pendulum"? or what a pendulum does?

S: [Gives simple description]

T: Please elaborate on this description

"Now," Mike asked. "What are your questions worth investigating?"

Students worked at their tables generating ten or fifteen questions about the simple system and its multiple variables or elements. Mike elicited them all and then challenged students "to identify one question you wish to answer. Then develop your hypothesis, keeping in mind the different variables we have identified."

Eventually, Mike had them work, for sake of economy of effort and maximum learning outcome from this one simple system, on an hypothesis around this question: "How does _____ (length and weight) of pendulum affect its period?"

Students then conducted their own experiments, made observations, collected data and started learning how to analyze such data. For example, there would always be multiple representations, by graph, mathematical equation, written word and the model itself.

Physics teachers will recognize a "standard" way of introducing students to the laws of physics, through analysis of simple systems. But I wonder what those of us who are not physics teachers find in Mike's way of introducing his students to what one physics teacher told me was "learning how the world works." Indeed, several students whom I interviewed for this project would refer to this explanation when asked why they liked the subject: "I like knowing how things work."

 ## Reflective Pause

What elements do we find here that are transferable into any subject?

Using Model Experiences to Commence Instruction

One thing I've learned from being a humanities teacher in "Mr. Z's" class is the power of the models he used. Here we've seen how he used the simple pendulum system to set up students for how they would be engaging complex phenomena within physics.

I use the word "model" here as a noun, a representation of reality. One researcher has defined models as "partial and inadequate ways of imagining what is not observable" (Barbour, 1974, 2013, p. 69).

This could be a small airplane, a much larger bridge or power plant, a wind tunnel or a representation of the solar system.

A model can also be a visual, a picture or diagram to show relationships, like a management chart.

Some models are analogical, as when we compare the workings of an atom to billiard balls crashing into each other or (older) to our planetary system. A model of the universe showing Einstein's theory of gravity as the bending by mass of space is constructed of a large piece of flexible fabric with a large object in the middle—representing the Sun, one that would draw objects (like planets) revolving about it toward the center.

Language Arts

We can use model poems, plays, essays and the like to represent an era or the best of an artist's work. We might start a unit with an analysis of one of Wordsworth's poems as a "model" of Romantic or Lake District poetry. For example, we might use Wordsworth's most famous poem as a model:

> I wandered lonely as a cloud
> That floats on high o'er vales and hills,
> When all at once I saw a crowd,
> A host of golden daffodils;
> Beside the lake, beneath the trees,
> Fluttering and dancing in the breeze . . .
>   (published 1807)

How is this poem like a pendulum?

It has elements within it that make it into a good example of Romantic poetry: emphasis on the individual, love of nature—retreat from city life, figurative language—simile, metaphor, personification, expressions of feelings—longing, melancholy, introspection . . . and, of course, powerful use of imagination in imagery and, perhaps, rebellion . . .

Where can we go from these identifications?

1. Use this as a set of criteria with which to analyze other examples, compare with Victorian and/or contemporary poetry.

2. Play "What if?" we modified, say, the emphasis on an individual's point of view, or the focus on nature.

3. Imitate Romantic poetry and then modify it.

4. Develop further students' skills with analyzing poetic selections.

History

In history we can select any historical conflict, say, the American Revolution, with the driving question, "How representative of revolutions was our fight for freedom? What were the key drivers, motivators, social conditions that fostered it, opponents and their reasons, major players, spark to set it going, how it proceeded and with what results?" (See Chapter 5 history example.)

We may find in analyzing other revolutions—Russian and French—that there were significant differences. We should be able, for example, to identify a variety of motivating factors: economic interests, financial needs, rights and privileges of citizens in different classes or economic strata.

Mathematics

In mathematics, here's a model problem in geometry, algebra of trigonometry. We can proceed as with the poem to identify major elements: givens, what's asked for, similarities to previously solved problems, relevant algorithms with which to solve, unstated assumptions needing to be questioned . . .

As before, we can then play the "What if?" game of asking, "Suppose we were to modify this variable/number here? How would that change our approach? Our outcome?"

And, we can learn about how we go about analyzing complex problems by challenging students with "What questions do we need to ask about this problem in order understand it?" This is the kind of analytic question too seldom asked in American education according to Harold Stevenson (1994). We're too busy teaching students how to learn a formula and plug numbers into same to get the right answer. It's the analysis that really counts.

Music

In music, we'll play a Chopin sonata or ballad as a model of that genre. Then ask, "What do you observe about this piece, musically? What do you think are the important elements? Any resemblances to the Wordsworth poem 'I wandered lonely as a cloud . . .'"?

How do these elements change within different musical genres of the same composer?

How do they differ, for example, from a Mozart or Beethoven sonata?

Sports

In sports, we'll look at how several pitchers with over 300 wins threw the ball, looking for characteristics of successful hurlers. Or we might do the same for players with over 3,000 hits or over 500 home runs. What are the elements of success? How do they differ?

Examine the moves of successful football, soccer or basketball players. What are the elements of their on-the-field/court success? Why can they serve as models?

What Mike did with the pendulum can be replicated in any subject. He took a model of a simple system and then provided students with a way of analyzing complex phenomena in the future.

Later in the semester Mr. Z would use motion sensors as models to depict laws of motion, carts racing toward each other, and a wheeled vehicle on a plane being pulled by weights dropping from two pulleys, and catapults as indicators of force, mass, trajectory, distance and acceleration. All served as models.

We as educators know that almost everything we do with our students (and children) serves as a model for imitation. It is not only our demeanor and behavior in front of the class, but the very artifacts and elements of the curriculum—the problematic and artistic exemplars—that also serve to guide our thinking.

Observe, Think and Question

When confronting them with the pendulum, Mike introduced them to a way of analyzing it. First, Describe what you see. This requires that we become close observers of the system.

As students are observing, perhaps jotting down notes, they are, of course, thinking, reflecting on what they already know about this simple system, other systems or any of the components. Maybe it reminded somebody of the pendulum in a large grandfather clock. Or a children's toy operating under similar principles.

And, Mike concluded this phase by challenging them to pose questions of interest.

Why do this? Why ask students to pose their own questions?

What do their questions have to do with interest, motivation, engagement and thinking like scientists? It should be obvious what students asking their own questions does for classroom dynamics. It's the entire basis of an inquiry-based curriculum, where students' questions can be what drives the curriculum as structured by the essential questions the teacher has laid out. Sometimes the two will even coincide. See Chapter Ten on social studies using the C3 curriculum model of inquiry.

And, the closer we examine something, the more likely we are to notice what's going on, say in a Thomas Cole or J.M.W. Turner painting. (How many times have I walked by at the Metropolitan Museum of Art without spending the time to take in all the artist has presented in his masterfully organized presentation of a Hudson River (NY) scene or of ships in the harbor!)

Observe, *think* and *question* is one of those thinking patterns or routines we can learn so that it just becomes part of how we engage life situations. Don't draw hasty conclusions! Stop, observe, see what's going on, get the facts first. (How often have people in public life made hasty proclamations without first obtaining the facts! To some it doesn't seem to matter much, sadly.)

Power of Students Collaborating with Each Other

Daily in most observed classrooms I saw the value of students collaborating with each other. This attests to the efficacy of students working together. As I'll note below from one of Mike's students during one of her teaching episodes, "We, students, see things differently from the teacher."

Why is this practice so effective?

1. Students have an audience for their ideas.
2. Having this audience means they are receiving recognition and this translates into engagement.
3. They do see the subject and its challenges differently from an adult.
4. In a small group we can get immediate feedback on our tentative ideas and questions. I attribute working in collegial small groups in graduate school with helping me overcome apprehensions about asking questions in a large group—everybody knows the answer . . . too simple . . .
5. There's a long record of the efficacy of small group peer instruction. What I see in these classrooms is students talking, responding, asking questions, discussing, debating, clearing up their misconceptions. When the sessions are over, we ask for large group sharing and here's where any lingering misconceptions are remediated.

Students' Choice and Control over Material

It should come as no surprise to anybody that two of the key elements in a very engaged classroom are students having partial control of learning outcomes and that this results from their having options and choices to make. Some choices we make from suggestions by our teachers, while others we imagine for ourselves.

One Eighth Grade language arts teacher in Catalina Foothills, AZ, Pat Burrows, studied organizational development in a master's degree program and noted that history and research tells us that, if we want people to have a "buy in," we should share control with them to some degree. We never relinquish total control of our learning environments, but we do offer students opportunities to make decisions about the nature of content and how they wish to share findings at certain times along the way.

> Bottom line here . . . if my students do not feel that they have any power when it comes to what and how they learn, they don't "own" their learning and become "bystanders." (Barell, 2012, p. 217)

And research confirms our consideration: "When students make choices about their own learning, their engagement and achievement increases." (Davies, 2007, p. 34)

For example, students in physics had choices over the following content areas: which questions to research (through hypotheses and experiments) with the pendulum; use of motion sensors in constant velocity problems; making quantitative predictions about objects that experience "angled forces" (resulting in the Force Diagrams); questions about catapults; and, ultimately, over their deeper and long-term research studies conducted with a faculty sponsor.

In Stephen Lazar's history class students had a very unusual set of choices: which recent current events to study in depth. They chose the Crimean crisis. From brief research into what was occurring (Russia annexed Crimea in March, 2014), they generated their own areas of interest with which to study the history of this situation in greater depth (histories of the leaders, Ukrainian politics and history, the Russian Revolution . . . and more). Steve, thus, modeled how historians analyze conflicts.

In Laura Mourino's Algebra 2 class students selected their own authentic life situations with which to do statistical analyses, e.g. crime, teenage pregnancies, attending college . . .

In language arts, students make choices about content to study within a novel or short story unit; they chose scenes to dramatize within *Macbeth* or *Twelfth Night* and they chose which questions to discuss based upon entries within their inquiry journals from the evening's readings of texts.

In all these classes, students are making choices, ones that surely enhance their stake in their own successes.

Presentations to Classmates and Receiving Feedback

As we shall see in Tim Obergefell's social studies classes (Chapter 10), two of the aspects of being defensive coordinator of a winning football team in Sandusky, OH, are making authentic presentations and receiving immediate feedback. Because his is a One-to-One school each student had her own computer in the field and was constantly sending him notes on her research—findings, failures and new questions—to which he could give almost immediate feedback.

Students in science are constantly figuring out problems in small groups, doing their work on white boards, sharing their findings with classmates in Walk-Abouts (students move from station to station) and then sharing with everybody. Here is where they get immediate feedback from their peers, another element of a winning sports team.

Authenticity

We often think of an "authentic" learning experience as described by Fred Newmann and his associates as engaging students in what adult professionals do in life:

> intellectual accomplishments that are worthwhile, significant, and meaningful, such as those undertaken by successful adults: scientists, musicians, business entrepreneurs, politicians, crafts people, attorneys, novelists, physicians, designers and so on. (1996, p. 26)

How does analyzing the system of a poem or the circulatory system relate to what "successful adults" do? We all can more effectively learn about complex systems/phenomena by having an organized, well-structured way of approaching them: observe, think, question, hypothesize, experiment, note results and draw conclusions.

This approach is also the essence of conducting "authentic" work in the various disciplines, relating to what people in that subject do.

Probing for Deep Understanding

All teachers ask questions to probe students' understanding of ideas they are expressing:

> What leads you to this conclusion?

> Please explain your thinking here.

How did you arrive at that answer/response?

How would you compare this historical event with another you know of?

How might we express this another way? (Use any art form to express the meaning you see/feel in this event, poem, picture . . .)

There is a special question that probably dates back to Plato's *Dialogues* in which Socrates constantly questions Athenian citizens about the nature of good government and the life well lived.

Surely, he asked these young men the "What if we do this?" kind of question.

In all classes where students are providing answers, we ask these kinds of "What if?" or "Suppose we did this?" kind of question that challenges them to manipulate one or more variables within the situation under discussion:

"What if Macbeth/Hamlet were the leader of Russia (any country) today?"

"Suppose you change the kinds of batteries we use in an iPhone?" (See Chapter Eleven)

"Imagine that Leonardo had painted 'Starry Night'? How would it be different?"

"What if Raskolnikov (protagonist of Dostoevsky's *Crime and Punishment*) came before Judge Judy or any other famous contemporary prosecutor?"

In each instance students require a firm understanding of the given situation as well as the other elements/personalities/variables we are introducing to respond logically to these forays into imaginative thinking.

Openness to Inquiry

We can consider inquiry as the platform from which we launch our own investigations. All new knowledge commences with questions, and students' questions, as we noted above, tap into their own background and serve as a highly motivating factor (if we pursue them).

The "Vision of the Graduate" at Greenwich, CT, high school notes that in addition to students learning traditional content (major concepts, relationships, principles), they want students to "be able to pose and pursue substantive questions."

What follows this posing of "substantive questions" is, of course, the list of 21st century skills, problem solving, critical/creative/reflective thinking, working collaboratively, empathy for and a sense of moral commitment to others. (See Chapter One.)

Conclusion

In this century, as in any other, good instruction depends upon so many factors and what we have listed above should be high on anybody's list.

Of course, we also want to be deeply involved in our subjects, to have a tremendous amount of enthusiasm for what we teach.

Finally, we should recognize that students make choices every day, in every class—to commit themselves wholeheartedly (or not!) during this time to learning what we are engaged in for this day.

Students often make poor choices in class—to be off task, to play around with others, to ask annoying off-topic questions—and they realize the consequences.

Modeling, observing and asking good questions are ways to engage students so that they wish to participate throughout the units of instruction. They deserve these kinds of opportunities, rather than just sitting back and maybe taking notes.

Application

1. How do you use the common elements mentioned herein: presenting models, peer critique and problem solving, close observations and questioning?

2. Which behaviors do you consciously model for students and why?

3. Wherein do you foster students' making and being responsible for choices within the curriculum: problems to solve? projects to undertake? ways of presenting to peers?

4. How do you and students probe each other for deep understandings?

5. How would you modify a previous unit (or plan a new one) to include some of these common threads within it?

References

Barbour, I. (1974, 2013) *Myths, Models and Paradigms*. New York: HarperOne.
Barell, J. (2012) *How Do We Know They're Getting Better? Assessment for 21st century minds, K–8*. Thousand Oaks, CA: Corwin Press.

Davies, A. (2007) "Involving students in the classroom assessment process." In D. Reeves (Ed.), *Ahead of the Curve: The power of assessment to transform teaching and learning*. Bloomington, IN: Solution Tree Press, pp. 31–58.

Newmann, F., & associates (1996) *Authentic Achievement—Restructuring schools for intellectual quality*. San Francisco, CA: Jossey-Bass.

Stevenson, H. (1994) *The Learning Gap: Why our schools are failing and what we can learn from Japanese and Chinese education*. New York: Simon and Schuster.

Chapter 7

Nurturing Imaginative Behavior

"Riding along a Ray of Light"

Most of us know of Einstein's very famous thought experiments ("Gedanken") where he imagined a situation, perhaps impossible or improbable to witness or, indeed, execute, in reality. These experiments posed questions stemming from his deep curiosity about nature, and the results were often startling.

For example, he asked himself this question: "What if I rode along a ray of light. What would I observe if I turned around and looked behind me?"

Now, we know this would be impossible, for a human to travel at 186,000 miles per second, the speed of light in a vacuum.

I have always been intrigued by this question (Barell, 1980) because of its consequences. Einstein reasoned from this question that light traveled at a uniform speed in all directions and its speed was not, therefore, affected by our own travel through space—on planet Earth.

This is a most powerful and imaginative question.

Why so?

Because the answer that Einstein developed resulted in the Special Theory of Relativity (1905): the speed of light is constant; space and time are not absolutes and energy and matter are related in the now famous equation $E = mc^2$.

How did he arrive at this revolutionary set of conclusions?

By using his imagination, thinking as "more or less in clear images" (Einstein, 1955).

He leapt the boundaries of logic and concrete reality to project himself into space and saw vividly in his mind (imagination) the picture of his riding along this ray of light and turning around.

When I sit down to write a long story I use the same approach: envisioning characters in a setting within a created situation and attempting to figure out what they will do—also by using "clear images" that take me away, often far, far away, from my workspace here in New York City.

When David Sherrin challenges his history students to dramatize how the wily Spaniards led by Cortez plotted to lure the Aztec chieftain Montezuma into their "protective custody" for purposes of stealing all his gold, these students are projecting themselves back into history and, with sufficient background knowledge, they are able to imagine themselves as either native Americans or the invading conquistadores. They are seeing themselves as history makers.

These are two of many aspects of imaginative thinking. Here's a more complete list:

1. Thinking in "more or less clear images" (Einstein), Vizualization.

2. Projecting ourselves into situations far removed from our current reality, in space, time, galaxy, universe or gender—acting out novel situations. Scientists have asked, "What if I were an electron? a bacterium?"

3. Asking "What if?" questions that challenge given realities and assumptions.

4. Creating models and metaphors—the atom as a solar system in miniature (Bohr).

5. Projecting consequences beyond the immediate present.

6. Challenging unstated assumptions.

7. Shifting or re-orienting to a different point of view or perspective.

8. Redefining an existing problem.

9. Designing a new product.

As you can see, imaginative thinking to me is more than "creativity." Creative thinking I often associate with problem solving and attempting to find novel solutions to concrete problems through experiences such as brainstorming (see Osborne, 1953). Such is the case with Velcro, the iPhone's touchscreen capability, and skate/snow boards. All reflect innovative ways of dressing, communicating and traveling. In the case of Velcro, it required imagining the burrs that stuck onto George de Mestral's coat during a walk in the woods as an alternative way to buckling, lacing and tying up one's clothes and shoes.

Imaginative thinking, as the poet Emily Dickinson noted, takes us "lands away" from the sluggish Earth upon which we stand at the moment, freeing up our senses to experience lives both real and invented in strange, captivating and transcendent fashions.

Why Is Imaginative Thinking Important?

Basis for Formal Thinking

We could say that our schools should foster imaginative thinking, because Einstein revolutionized our view of the cosmos and gave us lasers, black holes and a new view of gravity as the bending of space by large masses. But this would certainly be insufficient.

No, I suggest that imaginative thinking is vital for upper elementary, middle and high school students because they are growing and developing new mental capabilities. That is, their physical, emotional and mental development is providing them with the foundation to engage in all the above-numerated aspects of imaginative thinking.

We recall how Piaget defined "Formal Operational Thought," as engaging in more abstract kinds of reasoning that transcend the given, concrete and immediate realities before us (see Chapter Three).

Imaginative thinking is part of this and, we might say, imaginative thinking empowers or enables formal operational thought. It is reasonable to say that "formal thinking" is, indeed, akin to imaginative thinking. An adolescent capable of formal operational thinking should be able to engage in all aspects of imaginative thinking, given, of course, sufficient background knowledge in any given subject.

We saw, for example, in Chapter Three that the Peel Test of Contingency Thinking reveals those respondents who can transcend the limited number of facts about the airplane's crashing into the sky-ride cable. It takes imaginative thinking to create or "to see" the contingent possibilities: foul weather, poor charts, pilot illness, aircraft malfunction, being at war and the like. Students whose thinking has matured to enable them to envision these possibilities have liberated their thinking from the facts in the case, to project a wide variety of intriguing possibilities.

Essential for Deep Understanding

Another reason why we should be fostering imaginative thinking in all of our classes from upper elementary school (and perhaps earlier!) through high school and beyond is that imaginative thinking is key to approaching deep understanding of the content we are studying.

If we wish to understand how variables are manipulated in science—say in a chemical bond or in velocity–time graphs in physics—or in humanities—becoming Macbeth, President Jefferson or the Romantic poets—we need to create "more or less clear images," project ourselves bodily (imaginatively) into new spaces and roles, into lyrics ("A poet is a nightingale . . ." wrote Shelley) and into alternative realities (universes).

Just to understand how rectangles become triangles requires our creating pictures in our minds, unless we are able to cut the former on the diagonal and work with these objects.

Imaginative thinking is what enables us to lift our minds above and beyond the concrete givens of any situation (the swinging pendulum, the date 1776) and work with all elements and facets thereof. We're identifying the significant variables (time, space, persons, key elements therein), playing with them in our minds.

When Mike Zitolo in Physics 1 challenges his students to ask what he calls "Pushing Questions" ("What if?" "Why?" "Suppose?") about the recently conducted experiment with the pendulum, he's asking them to take flight from what they've calculated to imagine how the important variables might interact in a new formulation. For example, "What if you doubled the length of the string, raised the level of the pendulum holder and kept the weight constant?"

When we challenge our students with these kinds of "What if?" questions we are, in effect, taking the measure of the depth and quality of their understanding of, in this case, how the pendulum illustrates various factors and forces. If students cannot play with these variables in their minds and figure out how they are related, then they might not understand the situation in all its complexity—in science as well as in the humanities.

Tweeting *Macbeth*

And, I have seen outstanding educators like Hannah Magnan use contemporary technology to engage students mentally and emotionally in their understanding of *Macbeth* by reading the text of a certain scene and then formulating 144-character messages to send on Twitter to classmates. This required not only close reading, plot and character development comprehension, but also asking them to distill their analysis into brief, pithy and significant messages that worked together to move the action of the play forward and use a new vernacular to appeal to a specific audience. A few examples follow, each preceded with the original text:

Original Text

MACBETH:
Is this a dagger which I see before me,
The handle toward my hand? Come, let me clutch thee.

I have thee not, and yet I see thee still.
. . . Thou sure and firm-set earth,
Hear not my steps, which way they walk, for fear
Thy very stones prate of my whereabout,
And take the present horror from the time,
Which now suits with it.

Tweets

Macbeth: #ThatAwkwardMoment when you're not sure if the dagger in front of you is real #idowhatthevoicestellme

Macbeth: It's so quiet . . . I guess that's for the best considering what I'm about to do. #murderythoughts #pindrop

Hannah's approach has helped students more deeply understand the Shakespearean tragedy by virtue of having to read, interpret and compose with three different languages: Shakespearean prose, contemporary English and Twitterese.

Original Text

MACBETH
Whence is that knocking?
How is't with me, when every noise appalls me?
What hands are here? ha! they pluck out mine eyes.
Will all great Neptune's ocean wash this blood
Clean from my hand? No, this my hand will rather
The multitudinous seas incarnadine,
Making the green one red.
Enter LADY [MACBETH].
LADY MACBETH
My hands are of your colour; but I shame
To wear a heart so white. (Knock.) I hear a knocking
At the south entry: retire we to our chamber;
A little water clears us of this deed:
How easy is it, then! Your constancy
Hath left you unattended. (Knock.) Hark! more knocking.
Get on your nightgown, lest occasion call us,
And show us to be watchers. Be not lost
So poorly in your thoughts.
MACBETH
To know my deed, 'twere best not know myself.

Moving from What to *What If?*

(Knock.)
Wake Duncan with thy knocking! I would thou couldst!
PORTER
Here's a knocking indeed! If a man were porter of hell-gate, he
should have old turning the key . . . Come in time, have napkins
enough about you, here you'll sweat for 't . . .
PORTER
'Faith sir, we were carousing till the second cock. And drink, sir, is
a great provoker of three things.
MACDUFF
What three things does drink especially provoke?
PORTER
Marry, sir, nose-painting, sleep, and urine. Lechery, sir, it provokes
and unprovokes. It provokes the desire, but it takes away the
performance. Therefore, much drink may be said to be an
equivocator with lechery. It makes him, and it mars him; it sets
him on, and it takes him off; it persuades him, and disheartens
him; makes him stand to and not stand to; in conclusion,
equivocates him in a sleep, and, giving him the lie, leaves him.

Tweets

Macbeth: I just heard a knocking . . . man, every noise freaks me out
right now!
   Lady Macbeth: Quick! @Macbeth Look normal. #howsmyhair
#innocentflower
   Porter: Dude, I'm up. I'm the porter of hell's gate.
Cmon in. Ur gonna sweat a lot. #axespray #alsoimdrunk
#nosepaintingsleepandurine [This is a student's original Tweet]

Original Text

ROSS
Ah! good father,
Thou seest, the heavens, as troubled with man's act,
Threaten his bloody stage: by the clock 'tis day,
And yet dark night strangles the travelling lamp.
Is't night's predominance, or the day's shame,
That darkness does the face of earth entomb,
When living light should kiss it?
OLD MAN
'Tis unnatural,
Even like the deed that's done. On Tuesday last,

A falcon, towering in her pride of place,
Was by a mousing owl hawk'd at and kill'd.
ROSS
And Duncan's horses,—a thing most
strange and certain,—
Beauteous and swift, the minions of their race,
Turn'd wild in nature, broke their stalls, flung out,
Contending 'gainst obedience, as they would
Make war with mankind.

                                    (Act II, Scene IV)

Tweet

Ross: #tfln When there's a bunch of tornadoes and your horses
go all cannibal during an eclipse while birds drop from the sky.
#apocalypsemuch

We might say that moving through all three languages from Shakespeare
to Twitterese involves imaginatively going beyond the givens, creating a
startling and novel declaration: "horses go all cannibal . . ."

Twitter represents a different means of communicating, compressed as
is poetry and full of meaning. This is one of several new "literacies" for our
students, new modalities of communications.

Recent research (Gleason, 2015) suggests that our students use Twitter for
multiple purposes and we should pay attention to this growing phenomenon:

Young people demonstrated a wide variety of uses for Twitter,
including self-expression, communication, information-sharing,
friendship maintenance, and, simply for fun. As a social network,
Twitter supported young people's goals of friendship maintenance
through Twitter-specific practices of tweeting, retweeting,
hashtagging, mentioning and favoriting. The hashtag, in particular,
allowed participants to be part of the story . . . part of developing
communities of discourse and communications.

Gleason stresses that, for his study of adolescent use of Twitter, com-
municators paid attention to meanings, and grammar, to "make sure their
texts were intelligible (or, perhaps more importantly, 'relate-able') to their
followers—this included proof-reading tweets, eliminating typos, and revising texts" (p. 18).

Hannah's students have demonstrated that using Twitter is a way of
challenging their ability to think imaginatively, creatively, thus transcending
the ordinary bounds of discursive language.

Role-Playing and Mock Trials[1]

Have you ever witnessed students acting out the roles of Spanish Conquistadores "persuading" Montezuma to provide them, willingly (!), with a "room full of gold," as Cortez and his men did? When I visited David Sherrin's history class wherein these role-play simulations are acted out, I can see the students' delight in getting up, collaborating to make a plan (under David's guidance) and acting out their choices. Imagine the emotional charge from playing Montezuma and Cortez during the calculations that led to the conquest of the Mexican Empire.

Toward the end of the semester I journeyed over to Brooklyn's Municipal Courts to sit as a juror in a mock trial of an actual Nazi sympathizer and known anti-Semite, Julius Streicher. Students had spent days analyzing actual data from his life as a polemicist. They represented those prosecuting him for crimes against humanity and those defending him. I listened in as they framed questions for various witnesses testifying about his alleged "crimes."

Students' reflections following the Cortez, Luther and Nazi Holocaust units attest to the value for students of becoming agents, actors on the stage of history:

"It makes it all more real . . ."

"I always looked forward to this class."

"You can understand now the Nazi position." [Not that the student agreed with it!]

"Surely, the most exciting class of the year!"

Not passive recipients of massive amounts of data, but active participants in re-creating the history they are learning.

Imagination in the re-construction of a story, in the re-creation of history of the world stage, made all the more vivid by your being one of the actors, one of the history makers.

What gave me the most pleasure was structuring a freshman world literature class at Montclair State University around filming Dostoevsky's *Crime and Punishment*, complete with script writers, actors, directors, costume makers, set designers and lighting experts. Even if they were adhering primarily to Dostoevsky's intricate and gripping plot, they had to project, imagine and set themselves into nineteenth-century St. Petersburg with all the construction dust in the air and into the mind of an axe murderer. The class was always humming with planning, acting and reflecting. Was everybody joyously happy about these responsibilities? Perhaps not, but they seemed a lot more involved, socially, emotionally and intellectually. That's for certain.

"Imagine YOU ARE Richard Wright": Some Examples

Self-Projection

When I taught Richard Wright's *Black Boy* to New York City high school students, I did whatever I could to engage them imaginatively and emotionally. Here's one challenge I gave them after completing the reading:

> Imagine you are Richard Wright and you have moved to Chicago/New York during the 1930s. What would your life be like?

And then there was this:

> What if Richard Wright came upon the scene where you are living now, today. What would he find interesting? What would he want to do? Please give good reasons and examples based upon your knowledge of his life.

We once acted out this scene following the reading of *Macbeth*: "Suppose Macbeth came here to New York City. What would he do?" This might have been during a very contentious strike by the sanitation workers in the 1970s.

I can still recall some students claiming, "Macbeth wouldn't allow that! He'd take care of business like that, man!" Meaning he would do unto reluctant leaders what he did to poor King Duncan, probably slit his throat.

The idea here is to challenge students to imagine themselves inside the skin of a character in literature—or history.

At other times I've challenged teachers to do the following:

> Imagine you are one of the crew on Columbus' ship *Santa Maria*. You've just discovered that he's keeping two sets of logs—one secret with actual distances far from Spain and another, fictional account for the crew—being much closer to home. What would you do? (Barell, 1980)

Of course, some wish to deep-six Columbus, until others remind them that he's the only one with navigational skills on board.

Imaginative projection is fun, but requires good critical thinking. Your proposed actions must be presented with good reasons and solid, verifiable evidence drawn from the character's life. Once students who wanted to throw Columbus over the side of the *Santa Maria* realized he was the only capable navigator on board, they re-thought their solutions.

"What if?"

"What if Holden Caulfield dined with Dolly Parton?" This is a question I used to ask English teachers to consider as a model of a high-level intellectual challenge. Often times they would laugh or snicker. What a foolish question!

But then they would attempt to answer it and realized you had to know a lot about Holden Caulfield, his meetings with Roman Catholic nuns and their discussing the teaching of *Romeo and Juliet*, and, of course, about Miss Parton. Then it seemed not so frivolous, but became a test of students' understanding of Holden's nature.

Being a Chromosome

Nobel-Prize-winning biologist Joshua Lederberg describes how his imaginative faculties led him deep into the object of his studies:

> One needs the ability to strip to the essential attributes of some actor in a process, the ability to imagine oneself *inside* a biological situation; I literally had to able to think, for example, "What would it be like if I were one of the chemical pieces in a bacterial chromosome?"—and to try to understand what my environment was, try to know *where* I was, try to know when I was supposed to function in a certain way, and so forth. (Judson, 1980, p. 6)

Here is the witness of a renowned scientist proving the truth of what another scientist (and poet), Jacob Bronowski, affirmed, that

> science is as much a matter of imagination as poetry is . . . Science and literature, science and art, belong together as matched halves of what is unique in the human experience. (Bronowski, 1971)

Thus, in practical terms for all the subjects we investigate, "What if?"

"You were the tangent of a circle . . ."
"The native Americans had enslaved the European settlers/ conquerors . . ."
"Mozart had lived beyond age thirty-six . . ."
"Beethoven had not become deaf . . ."
"All the ice in Antarctica melted . . ."[2]

"All history had been written by women . . ."

"Harry Potter enlisted your help to solve a mystery . . ."

"Van Gogh had asked you to sell his 'Starry Night' to the Louvre Museum in Paris upon completing it—he needed the money for health care . . ."

In any subject we study we can play "What if?" games that challenge us to project, to imagine multiple possibilities that stretch our thinking, but games involving the hard critical analysis required. We identify and analyze the variables within and, through manipulating them, come to a deeper understanding of how they are all related.

Here's where proportional reasoning will enable our performance.

Poet Marianne Moore once wrote that "poetry is an imaginary garden with real toads in it."

In the cases above, the "real toads" are the key variables within the situation.

"Combinatory Play with Ideas"

Einstein described his thought process as being comprised of thinking "in more or less clear images . . ." A sort of "combinatory play with ideas."

This playing with ideas, images, pictures is what all artists and scientists do, from Watson and Crick and the process of discovering the DNA molecule to van Gogh's painting of "Starry Night" influenced by his early pencil sketches.

I see this kind of visualization play within Laura Maurino's introductory geometry class where she asked her Ninth Graders to figure out the dimensions of a rectangle created from a triangle. Laura gave each of her students a figure to investigate.

David was given an isosceles triangle with congruent sides measured 13 inches and whose base measured 10 inches. David cut the triangle in half and reassembled it into a rectangle. What is the perimeter of the rectangle David formed?

This is the problem wherein Jose claimed within three seconds, "I can't do this!"

Eventually, he was coaching others in how to find a solution.

At one point Laura said to her students working collaboratively at their separate tables, "The reason you were messing up is that you weren't visualizing it." Not creating those pictures, images in your mind and playing with them.

To solve this, students required knowledge of the Pythagorean theorem ($a^2 + b^2 = c^2$).

This is the kind of mental manipulation we all engage in (or, at least those of us of a certain age) during the SAT exams, rotating geometric figures problems. Some of Laura's students weren't good at it, and, finally, had to create a paper model and figure it out from conjoining the two pieces to form a rectangle.

Taking a Point of View

It is said of President Ronald Reagan that he changed the course of the Cold War by asking a question different from the one that had controlled US foreign policy since the days following the famous essay by Ambassador George F. Kennan—establishing the "containment policy." The question resulting from Kennan's thesis was "How do we contain the imperialistic Soviet Union?" Thus, the Cold War strategy was one of keeping the hungry Soviet bear safely within its own borders.

But President Reagan asked a different question: "How do we defeat Communism and the Soviet Union?" This shift in point of view, of perspective, launched a massive arms build up that some observers say helped deepen the economic crisis within the Soviet Union, unable to keep up with our spending.

Taking a Different Perspective

Sometimes, therefore, our imagination says to us, "What's a different way of looking at this problem or situation?" In effect, we are redefining the problem.

Hannah Magnan is a teacher full of experimental zest and determination, willing to stretch her students' thinking and feeling into a wide variety of dimensions.

Here's what she challenged them to do with *Macbeth*:

> Much of *Macbeth* focuses on an inability to know the truth of a situation based on how it appears. Many times, characters either erroneously assess situations based on appearances and faulty judgments, or they intentionally give false impressions.[3] Later, they reflect on their experiences with [often regretful] clarity, wishing they had known what the future held. Your assignment will be to compose a creative exploration of this concept in your own personal narrative.

She then challenged students to select a childhood photo "which has a story behind it that is not immediately obvious from the picture itself . . ." "Describe the picture. Write the story in the photo. Write the epilogue of each character in the story."

Finally, she asked them to

> write a one page reflection that connects your narrative to the play . . . How did this process [of reflection] help you understand the characters' conflicts, thought processes, and developments or the playwright better? What did you do to complete this assignment that they did? What was their result? Yours?

How, would you say, has Hannah challenged her students to engage in imaginative thinking?

When I first read this assignment I wondered how it came into being. Hannah shared with me her own story, also shared with her students, of a family photo:

> They are almost indistinguishable: the two blue-pale little girls captured breaking ground for their sand palaces.

A brave telling of childhood memories.

This assignment still intrigues me, because I see here much more than students' projecting themselves into *Macbeth* through critical comparison and contrast. Hannah has asked them to play with point of view: "You may want to shift to first person and past tense . . ." In writing the epilogue of this story, "You should probably switch to the future tense as you are referring to a point in the future from when the photo was taken . . ."

Would this person have become the "person they became (in your epilogue) if they had known what the future held?"

It's hard for me now to keep all these possibilities in mind—shifting perspectives and time frames, visualization of past and future, definitely skills requiring imaginative projection and playing with possibilities. These foundational imaginative processes enable the critical analysis Hannah requires: compare your life experiences with those found within Shakespeare, learn to share human experiences, if not empathize, with his deeply flawed characters.

Not an easy task and far more complex than when I used to ask my New York City street kids to imagine Macbeth taking the place of Mayor John Lindsay or Sanitation leader Michael Quinn.

Draw Your Understanding

One of my most imaginative assignments came as a culmination to the study of *Othello*: "Use any created form to reflect your understanding of the themes and characters in *Othello*. Justify your choices in writing."

I received full-length poem about Desdemona.

And, a sonata for viola played for the entire class during presentations on an eighteenth-century instrument.[4]

Similarly, Andy Snyder asked his history class studying slavery to draw their understandings of various events in the life of Frederick Douglass. (See eResources for *Moving from* What *to* What If? www.routledge. com/9781138998612/. Here you will find student's drawings together with Andy's and the student's reflections on the process.)

Obviously, Andy is challenging their ability to imagine, to vizualize, to put themselves into history, take a different point of view. And from these drawings we have a reasonable assessment of students' understandings of the characters in this historical drama.

Models/Metaphors

A theme in literature is like "getting to the middle of an artichoke. You get to the middle and see what made all the leaves. That is the root of it" (LaTanya).

This is the challenge we presented to high school students in Newark, NJ, during a project designed to capture the depth and quality of their understanding of major processes required for understanding literature: create your own model or metaphor of a significant concept within the subject. Teachers identified important concepts: theme, imperialism, factoring . . . Students created their own models. The premise here was that what we create is far more meaningful than what somebody else has presented to us. And we'll remember it longer.

In history, "Imperialism is like a shark. A shark seems to own or have power over less powerful fish . . ."

"Colonialism is a pimp who takes all the money . . ."

"Autocracy is a game of 'Simon Says' . . ."

"Democracy is a parking lot . . ."[5]

"A coup d-état is a cancer . . ."

In math, "Factorization is like slicing a cake and eating it piece by piece" (Barell & Oxman, 1984, p. 13).

What has been fascinating to me about these students' metaphors is the clarity of their thinking: analyzing "Theme" to identify what is significant and then imaginatively scanning their prior knowledge to find a suitable match like the artichoke.

Creating metaphors and models does indeed require imaginative play with objects, creating pictures in our mind's eye and then engaging in the critical thinking tasks of comparing/contrasting to find an appropriate fit. Does peeling an artichoke give us a vivid picture of what it's like for students to dig down through all the characters, lines of prose, visual images and symbols to get at "the root" or theme of the work of art?

Hannah Arendt (1977) noted that "analogies, metaphors and emblems are the threads by which the mind holds onto the world . . . moreover, in the thinking process they serve as models to give us our bearings . . ."

Our imagination creates these "threads" or anchors by which we create meaning within our complex world. They aren't always good or accurately representative of the hidden realities, say of the atom. I learned that the atom was like a miniature solar system. Now we do not use that model created first by Niels Bohr. Today, it's more complex. As one high school student wrote, the atom and the constantly shifting electrons are more like cars at a parking garage, moving in and out of various slots close or far away from the central core—the nucleus.

These "threads" allow us to hold onto the world, but they also, if created by students themselves (rather than memorized from experts) reveal the depth and quality of students' understanding. Compare the parking lot metaphor with this one created by another high school student in the same class: "An atom is composed of a nucleus with proton and neutron and electrons moving about."

Which is the creative deeply understood representation and which the definition?

I would say LaTanya has an abiding understanding of "theme." The following year I asked her if she remembered that metaphor and, indeed, she did almost word-for-word.

Once, again here is the need for solid proportional reasoning to make these complicated comparisons, theme and artichoke, Hitler and Kaiser Wilhelm II.

How Do We Assess Imaginative Thinking?

Take a clue from the responses to students creating metaphors and models about the construction of the atom:

> An atom is composed of a nucleus with protons and neutrons and electrons moving about it.

An atom is like a parking lot . . . The center is composed of protons and neutrons and all the cars are vying for position at different levels (of energy) to move closer to this center.

What differences do you see?

One is a strict definition, right from the textbook.

The second has created a visual image—of a parking lot—one with specific characteristics. We can judge this model by the "fit" of the characteristics to that which we know from nuclear physics about the nature of the atom today. The imaginativeness might be judged by the distance from the definition, as with a parking lot, the elaboration of different features and, of course, its originality.[6]

We could use the same criteria to assess David Sherrin's students imagining themselves as Aztecs and Spaniards or as Martin Luther: who acted in accordance with history as it was written and who gave an innovative, never-before-seen/original performance. This might involve a novel approach to the problem, but one that can be thoroughly justified by its internal logic, or its inventive use of the facts at hand.

We can do the same with LaTanya's Theme is like "getting to the middle of an artichoke . . ." Check the fit of the description with accepted definitions of theme and then look for originality, flexibility (different point of view, which this certainly has!) and elaboration. The latter might come in students being able to logically justify their reasons for their creation.

As well, we can assess the degree of imaginativeness and understanding in the drawings from history in Andy Snyder's class using Torrance's (1974) characteristics of creativity: Originality, Fluency, Flexibility and Originality. Judging the originality of a drawing will, I suggest, be enhanced by asking each artist to explain her reasoning leading up to the final product. Did they copy from a book? Probably not, but where did the original ideas come from?

Similarly, we can assess students' abilities to visualize by their scores on SAT-type test items, ones I often found most challenging.

Conclusion

Jacob Bronowski once observed that "imagination is the opening of the system so it shows new connections" and in the learning experiences we have presented I think we can confirm his observation. Hannah Magnan has helped students see their own lives in ways they probably never thought of, starting with a childhood photograph and imagining their stories from different perspectives.

When we played our metaphoric games in Newark high schools we were challenging teachers to help students connect the content of their subjects to the lives they experienced beyond the classroom walls: that of food preparation, ocean life and the hardscrabble life on urban streets.

Having written this chapter I now have a greater appreciation for the importance of proportional reasoning for the development of our burgeoning imaginations.

To be human is to imagine, to think and see beyond, first the hills on the African savannah, and wonder "What lies yonder, out of sight?" To transport ourselves up into that collection of three stars in a downward pointing straight line that we see in the winter skies around New York—Orion's Belt—and, were we the early Greeks, to imagine a story of a hunter with a bow declaring himself the greatest hunter in the world.[7]

We can and should do more to foster this foundational set of processes, so significant for our growth and development as alive, purposeful and productive human beings.

Note a recent example from the 2015 Pulitzer Prize Novel *All The Light We Cannot See*, by Anthony Doerr:

> *The brain is locked in total darkness, of course, children*, says the voice. *It floats in a clear liquid inside the skull, never in the light. And yet, the world it constructs in the mind is full of light. It brims with color and movement. So how, children, does the brain, which lives without a spark of light, build for us a world full of light?* (2014, p. 58)

Indeed! Where did such an idea come from? How in working though the intricacies of this amazing story for five years did Anthony Doerr generate such a question, one that perhaps several neuroscientists had thought of, but not most of the reading public?

Application

1. How have you used imaginative thinking in your classrooms to provide another means of self-expression? Very often words escape us.

2. Where have you found examples of students' imaginative thinking in their work? How have you displayed or shared it with others in the class?

3. How might you evaluate their work? Advice: try it yourself first.

4. In planning your next unit, how might you enhance students' expressions of understanding by using one of these approaches of imaginative thinking?

5. What is the role of imaginative thinking in your subject? Why is it important? Do you agree with Bronowski that imagination is just as important in the sciences as in the humanities? Why?

Notes

1. See David Sherrin, *The Classes They Remember* (2015).
2. A question I posed while doing qualitative research of high school students thirty-five years ago, before it reflected the realities of global warming: West Antarctica ice sheets are melting whereas East Antarctica is becoming colder. *Playgrounds of Our Minds* (Barell, 1980).
3. "False face doth hide what false heart doth know."
4. See Barell, *Teaching for Thoughtfulness* (1995).
5. Leslie Jenkins, the teacher, asked about this comparison: "Each car in a lot has equal space, just as in a democracy all rights for people should be equal . . . In a parking lot everyone pays the same amount of money . . . so there is justice in both." Jenkins (1982). How do we represent with more power and influence?
6. We are here using E.P. Torrance's (1974) criteria for creativity: Originality; Fluency (number of ideas); Flexibility (different points of view reflected); and Elaboration of thought, confidence and expertise. Here are the 21st century skills we will encounter in several different classrooms.
7. Perhaps the Greeks were as fascinated with Orion as we are because it contains two of the brightest stars in the sky, Betelgeuse, a shoulder, and Rigel, a knee, together with the visible and very prominent stellar nursery, the Orion Nebula just below the belt. See http://apod.nasa.gov/apod/ap140408.html (accessed December, 2015).

References

Arendt, H. (1977) "Thinking—Reflections, Part II," *The New Yorker*, 28 November.
Barell, J. (1980) *Playgrounds of Our Minds*. New York: Teachers College Press.
Barell, J. (1995) *Teaching for Thoughtfulness: Classroom strategies to enhance intellectual development* (2nd edn). New York: Longman.
Barell, J., & Oxman, W. (1984) "Hi Heels and Walking Shadows: Metaphoric Thinking in Schools." Paper presented to the American Educational Research Association, New Orleans.
Bronowski, J. (1971) *The Identity of Man*. New York: Natural History Press.
Doerr, A. (2014) *All The Light We Cannot See*. New York: Scribner's.
Einstein, A. (1955) "A letter to Jacques Hadamard" in B. Ghiselin (Ed.) *The Creative Process*. New York: New American Library.
Gleason, B. (2015) "New Literacies Practices of Teenage Twitter Users," *Learning, Media and Technology*, on-line publication, 29 July.

Jenkins, L. (1982) "Teaching History with Creative Metaphors." Unpublished paper, Upper Montclair, NJ: Montclair State College (University) quoted in Barell (1995) .

Judson, H.F. (1980) *The Search for Solutions.* New York: Holt, Rinehart & Winston.

Osborne, A. (1953) *Applied Imagination.* New York: Scribner's.

Sherrin, D. (2015) *The Classes They Remember: Using role-plays and mock trials to bring social studies and English to life.* New York: Routledge.

Torrance, E.P. (1974) *Torrance Tests of Creative Thinking.* Bensenville, IL: Scholastic Testing Service, Inc.

Intermission

It is time to take a brief break in our discussions to set up what follows in the remaining chapters of this book.

Up to now I have been attempting to present the case for engaging our students in the highest levels of intellectual challenge, called "authentic work," and "problem-based learning."

What I also stressed is that within any one of the classes presented in subsequent chapters you will find these common elements woven throughout each of their classrooms:

Inquiry.

Students thinking at highest intellectual levels.

Setting our own goals for achievement.

Imaginative thinking beyond the boundaries.

Authentic work reflecting what adults do in the world.

Students making choices about what and how to learn.

Peer tutoring and sharing.

Modeling of teacher behaviors as well as instructional practices.

Rigorous assessments of students' growth over time from pre and summative assessments.

I list these again in order to encourage those who, like me, began a teaching career within one discipline—language arts. There is much for each of us to learn from visiting classrooms in science, math and social studies, a practice we know can enhance our own instructional confidence and expertise.

Chapters 8 and 9: Problem solving in civics and mathematics.

Chapters 10 and 11: Critical reasoning in argumentation and physics.

Chapter 12: Independent study on star formation in the Milky Way.

Chapter 13: District-level change and professional development toward authentic intellectual work.

Final Words from a graduate of these kinds of rigorously demanding programs.

Chapter 8

"Any Citizen Can Make a Change"

At the end of the project, I learned that any citizen can make a change.
(Sabrina's reflections on her own problem solving, 2013)

We might all agree that we wish our students to become educated so that by graduation from high school they possess Sabrina's awareness of the power of self-determination, grit and civic pride. Not all of us have opportunities such as those within Tim Obergefell's government class, but we all strive toward similar goals, that of fostering independence and collaborative problem-solving skills amongst all our students. The problems they will face upon leaving formal education are similar to those encountered by Tim's students: complex, messy and lending themselves to few easy solutions.

What Tim has done is to provide us with a model of How to accomplish these goals and make a difference in his students' lives.

The Nature of Problem Solving

In the government (including, especially, the military) we conduct what are called After Action Reviews following any significant operation. Here personnel ask three questions: "What did we attempt to achieve/our goals?" "What did we achieve?" and "How do we explain the difference between the two?" An additional and important question is, of course, "How do we improve?"

This model was developed by the military after the Vietnam War and is often used in government agencies as well as in business.

These questions help us define problem solving as the difference between the Ideal and the Real. If we conduct military operations, say the capture of a fortified position during a training exercise, and achieve a certain degree of success, afterward we would want to learn from the experience by comparing what we hoped to achieve with what, in reality, we did achieve.

So, a problem can be viewed as the difference between ideal conditions in any human endeavor and what the reality is. In mathematics, our goal is to discover the unknowns, to close the gap between unknown and known (or knowable).

In social studies we will be launching young students out into the community to identify their own problematic situations and figure out how to solve them.

STEM Goals

Tim's school, Perkins High School, has determined that one of their major curricular goals will be to promote STEM subjects: science, technology, engineering and mathematics.

Early documents from faculty planning reveal their concern for four major elements: Creativity, Collaboration, Critical Thinking and Communications. Within their documents you can see itemized aspects of different rubrics (see Appendix) focused on Creative Thinking, Collaboration and Problem Solving.

There was a strong emphasis on project-based/problem-based learning:

> Projects: Students will be creating (2–4) semester projects that
> will promote understanding of core subject areas (English, World
> Languages, Arts, Math, Economics, Science, Geography, History,
> Government and Civics). In addition to core subjects, projects focus
> on interdisciplinary themes of global awareness, with financial, civic,
> health literacy, and environmental literacies as related to P21 skills.

Tim's projects certainly encompass "civic literacy" and the skills of problem solving and critical thinking.

First Benchmark Assessment

How did Tim assess his students' approach to problems related to civics and how to get things done in government?

He presented several challenges in September. Each one was complex, open ended, authentic in terms of relating to issues within the school and community and allowed for multiple entry points or ways of analyzing it. Recall our definition of authentic intellectual work, as that dealing with real-to-life problem-solving performed by professionals beyond and within schools.

Here's one: "A community group would like to add sidewalks to a busy street in Sandusky. Explain the steps this group would have to take to make this happen."

In analyzing students' responses we can identify those who have a rather limited understanding of how to effect change in the community, one of the major curricular themes of Tim's course.

Lorraine: They would have to contact their local government and ask for permission and funding.

Grant: They would need to create a proposal then present the proposal to the city of Sandusky.

Madison: Contact city services. Come up with a plan for your sidewalk locations on a map. Propose your plan to the city council.

And there are those who cast a wider net, who have identified more of the complexities of this situation:

Abigail: The group would have to get all of the facts on how the sidewalks would improve the community. Then they'd have to convince the community and the local government with a detailed presentation. Through the local government and eventually to the state government, the sidewalks could be put in place.

Kerry: First they would have to research about that area. What accidents have happened before? Who will use the sidewalk? How much will it cost? Then with the information they will have to present to a court room to get it approved.

Robert: First, this group would have to figure out what all would be involved for putting in a sidewalk, as far as costs go, time involved, etc. Then they would have to take their information and present it to representatives in Sandusky, in attempt to persuade them into approving a plan to build sidewalks. Then, if they could get their government to approve the plan, sidewalks would be built.

Sarah: The community group would have to follow a certain number of steps for this to go through. They would have to brainstorm and think of ways that this would be beneficial for our community. After making sure they know reasons why getting sidewalks is a good idea, they would have to present to the township trustees of Perkins to get this approved.

Reflective Pause

Now, what differences do you see between the two groups of students and amongst those in the first group and those within the second?

In examining the first set of three here are some aspects worth considering:

1. Short responses, not very developed.

2. Simplistic in approach, meaning all you have to do is present a plan to authorities and that's it. Lorraine doesn't seem to require a plan, just go and ask and you shall receive. Major unstated assumptions about how government works.

3. No sense of history, need, alternatives, the change process.

But then if we examine the second set we find:

1. Lengthier, more fully developed responses. More time given to analyzing the problem.

2. More complex, containing more thought elements, factors in the change process: research; costs; plans/petitions/persuasion; knowledge of city government offices/roles; allocation of funds; and a change process required.

3. Notice that Kerry and Sarah have a sense of history: we need to find out what has transpired to create and justify such a need. Perhaps, they also realize that not all expressed "needs" are justified nor can be met at a certain time.

4. A far more complex process is involved: identifying needs, history and benefits together with costs.

What Tim has here is a spectrum from *Simple to More Complex* in terms of effecting community change. Students' responses may reveal, of course, lack of background knowledge; minimal interest in civic affairs; lack of interest in the challenge/problem itself and a rather concrete, simplistic approach to certain kinds of problems. Some may also reflect a lack of personal/group efficacy and control: there's nothing we can do about it, so why bother?

And they also reflect each student's cognitive development, the ability to think abstractly about a new situation with many elements and variables, reason proportionally, pose "What if?" questions about hidden assumptions. (See Chapter Three.)

Tim's Focus Is upon Government and Civics

Since I have not been in Sandusky to observe Tim's teaching (though we've Skyped on numerous occasions), I asked him to outline how he structured an introduction to government between the pre assessments and the first large-scale project Sabrina undertook. Here's what he wrote me in an email:

> The beginning of the year we have group and individual studies on political ideology and political philosophy. We create a small group video in support of either the Democrat or Republican parties. We have debates and discussions over ideology and what it means to be from a certain party. We then go into the discussion of federalism (states vs. federal) powers and how the powers of our government are divided and each have roles. This leads us into the Constitution powers and the Amendments (Documentary project 2014 here). Students are required to attend our board or trustee meetings every nine weeks in an outside activity assignment. This gives them a little bit of an idea of what goes on at the meetings. (Personal email, February 10, 2014)

Given this kind of background and preparation, Tim has laid out this major challenge for his juniors:

> In groups of 4 or less, students will decide on an issue and present their solution on the issue. All presentations will be given in front of community members. The best presentations will present to the governmental body (school board, business owner, principal, state or local govt.). Whose group will have the best idea? Can students better the community they live in? The project has to be realistic and capable of being implemented.

This is a long-term project reflecting STEM planning goals as specified at the end of this chapter.

You will notice how this problematic scenario (Chapter Two) closely resembles Tim's pre assessment benchmarks asking students how they would go about making changes to Sandusky's sidewalks. One of the benefits, of course, of having such a benchmark is for students to compare their initial thoughts with final reflections on the process. Sabrina initially thought that effecting such changes through government would be relatively easy. She quickly learned about the realities of how government at the local level (and higher levels) works.

Authentic Feedback

It is interesting to me that one of the aspects within this challenge is that of presenting findings before "community members." For Tim the need to share results with members in the community comes from his work as defensive coordinator of Perkins High School football team. When I asked him how being a coach affected his being a social studies teacher, he identified two processes: giving immediate feedback and performing in front of an authentic audience.

> Much as in coaching, I view myself as working with the student for common goals. Projects are open ended with student choice. I become a facilitator that helps students contact the right people, ask the right questions and provide critical feedback. In my projects we are both invested in the project and I bring an outside panel to provide feedback to the kids. *I've always thought students work their hardest in front of a crowd and thought that putting my students in front of the community panel would be very similar to a game like approach to a project.* I've seen unbelievable results by putting the final project in front of others. (Personal email, January, 2014, emphasis added)

When the school became a One-to-One school with each student having a laptop it was, of course, much easier for Tim to observe, monitor and evaluate students' progress as well as provide them with direct, timely feedback while they were out of class working in the field.

Students' Improvement

Tim concluded that his students had improved in the important areas of problem solving, critical thinking and learning how to manage time, resources and public speaking. As you will note, the data that led to these conclusions comes from these sources: 1. Teacher observations of small group problem solving; 2. Students' PowerPoint Presentations at the end of the project; 3. Students' on-going self-reflections on their own growth in inquiry journals; and 4. Parental reflections on their children's growth.

Figure 8.1 Rubric

Investigation (Problem Identification and Resolution): Presents a thorough and correct account of what is already known. Identifies the important confusions, uncertainties or contradictions surrounding the topic. Brings to light misconceptions or confusions that are commonly overlooked (Critical Analysis). Provides a logical and well-developed resolution to the confusions, uncertainties or contradictions.

Invention (Creative Thinking): Proposes a process or product that provides a unique solution to an unmet need. The proposed process or product reflects a high level of creativity. Sets out rigorous criteria well suited to the purpose of the invention. The student identifies only the highest achievable standards of quality as acceptable outcomes.

Inductive Reasoning (Intake of Information): Clearly and accurately identifies all relevant information from which to make inductions. The type of information selected reflects creative insight and a careful analysis of the situation.

Abstracting: How does the current complex situation extend, map out to other, similar situations? What connections can we observe?

Unlike results from so-called high stakes "bubble tests," what Tim observed is direct, immediate, related specifically to each student in the process and confirmed by the adults—teachers and parents—in the situation.

Tim's conclusions were fashioned based upon the district rubric (Figure 8.1).

Other projects included avoiding traffic accidents in front of a local McDonald's restaurant and improving the quality of basketball playing facilities in the town.

Induction and Inquiry

Tim wrote me in an email:

> To measure growth for students in inductive reasoning, I start with the initial brainstorming session and ask what would you change in our community? Kathryn: "I want to change safety in sports." Kathryn states "We interviewed doctor Strohl (our AD) and the local hospital." *I am measuring the types of questions that students ask at the beginning of the project and then compare that with their final evaluation.* (Personal email, January, 2014, emphasis added)

Realistic Solutions and Barriers

> I was able to watch Sabrina's group develop three of their own ideas.
> These solutions were all viable if students had unlimited money.
> Watching the students after each interview and researching their real
> solutions becomes more defined. In outside contact paper 1,
> Sabrina's questions start to change "What are some possible
> solutions? What would be the cost of fixing the intersection?"
> (Personal email from Tim, February, 2014)

The naive notion, as expressed in some pre tests, that you make a proposal, take it to local authorities and they approve it, is soon dashed on the rocks of hard-scrabble realities. In one of her project journal entries Sabrina wrote that she thought this project would be "way easier than [it turned out] to be."

As in life beyond the classroom, the problem solvers had to realize that the impediments to their easy solutions presented other problems: money, sewer maintenance, personal responsibility of drivers. They must consider, "Is this passing the buck?" These impediments might be considered the "confusions, uncertainties or contradictions" found in any human problem solving endeavor—the obstacles to overcome.

Tim's summative assessments of his students' progress using the rubric continue:

> The students' thinking starts to address the financial issues
> involved and brings in another problem that students have to solve
> as they realize county and business spending is limited. *I begin to see
> students that start to make realistic solutions with real-life barriers to their
> problem. The group starts with one problem but moves to a completely
> different issue with each interview.* (Personal email, February, 2014,
> emphasis added)

Tim was able to follow their thinking as they generated multiple solutions to the traffic accident problem in front of the McDonald's at the Sandusky Mall:

> Sabrina's group comes up with 3 ideas on their own: (1) "Red
> flashing light," (2) Paint, signs and right turn only lane. (3) Add a
> triangle. They start with questions to ask the outside contact.
> I view the students questions at the beginning "Is this intersection an
> issue?" "Do you see this as a problem?" The research they conduct is
> able to show statistics to prove that there is an accident problem 60%
> of the time at this intersection alone. They also run into the problem
> of the mall manager having a difficult time and resisting their idea.

These assessments are, again, direct, informal and relate to each student's progress. How can we trust them? They are derived from a well-established and accepted-by-all framework of what is to be judged (Figure 8.1). They are confirmed by the results obtained in each project—in this case real modifications to the traffic patterns in front of the McDonald's at the Sandusky Mall.

Parental Assessment

Tim not only challenged the students to assess themselves, he also conducted his own assessments in accordance with the rubrics presented above. But he went a step further. He elicited comments from parents of these students.

One parent whose son participated in the Concussion project wrote Tim this in an email:

> As a parent and as a teacher, I feel that the project was an extremely valuable experience for my son and Perkins' students. My son was interested in the project and took pride in his work. I appreciate the fact that he gained experience in communicating formally with school and community leaders. To see my son, who is generally a quiet young man, feel good about making a presentation is evidence of his growth and confidence that he has gained as a result of this project.

And, this parent is also a teacher:

> As a teacher, I appreciated the fact that I could show my Fourth Graders that Perkins High School students were listed on the agenda of the Perkins Township Trustees meeting to present their projects. This happened at the same time that I was teaching my students about government and how citizens can be a part of government and make a difference in their community. Thank you for the time you put into the development and management of this project!
> Julia Mack (Comment used with permission,
February 10, 2014)

To "feel good about making a presentation" is, indeed, a major accomplishment not only for a high school student, but also for many adults. "Glossophobia"—fear of speaking in public—is said to be a most common fear amongst adults.

And having models of assuming responsibility for your community surely is a major step toward educating all students to be willing and able to make a difference in the world.

Tim is educating his students to accept responsibility for their lives and to strive toward enhancing the quality of public life within the community.

Conclusion

In addition to working on problems of concussions, automobile accidents and recreational facilities (basketball courts), Tim's students have set their sights on improving sidewalk access to one of the country's largest theme roller-coast parks, Cedar Point. As of this writing (June, 2015) he advises me work is proceeding to follow students' lead.

And, one of his subsequent teams undertook to revamp Sandusky's baseball diamonds. Tim summarized students' end-of-term work:

> We have settled on replacing our 4 new baseball fields built at the Perkins High School location. We found out that shared costs between the township and the school provides much greater costs savings for the field. The drawings are currently being done by Maumee Turf Baseball. Most of the work has been carried on by myself since the students could only take it so far. The students actually came and watched me present their project to the township after I formed a group to research their project more deeply. We found government moves slowly and that projects must adapt to fit the government's wishes. After we get the drawings we will start the fundraising for the project as soon as next week. (Personal communication, June, 2015)

Value of Projects

Why is this kind of problem-based learning approach important? We've heard from experts like Fred Newmann and John Bransford. Once again, here's Sabrina, one of our local experts on her own learning:

> At the end of the project, *I learned that any citizen can make a change.* This project has helped me realize that even students can improve a problem in a community, which was unexpected. I honestly never knew that students could make a change until the panel told my group that we should keep pushing this intersection problem to make it more successful. The panel has motivated me to make a change. (Emphasis added)

Brandon, working on the baseball project, had similar self-assessments:

I learned that being a good citizen means taking an active role in one's community. It requires that when one sees a problem in a community to take an action to try and resolve it, no matter how trivial it might seem.

Brandon also had significant reflections on problem solving:

As far as myself, I've learned that sometimes I need to step back when I encounter a problem and analyze the entire situation before proceeding, otherwise I might just start to stress and not accomplish anything. I've learned that our project is much more involved than what it initially appears, and a lot of money needs to be factored when trying to figure out the finances. For working with my group, I've learned that communication is key when trying to solve problems. (Personal communications, June, 2015)

Problem solving in social studies is different from that in other subjects. In sciences and math, we very often have provable, predictable and convergent outcomes. But at the core they use very similar intellectual processes: identifying a problem, conducting research to gather information, question assumptions, analyze data critically and draw reasonable conclusions. Depending upon the nature of the problem to be solved, you will in the sciences and math have room for interpretations leading to varying results. (See Chapter Nine and Laura's benchmarks.)

Yet, each person's approach is unique, depending upon her background knowledge, comfort levels with reasoning abstractly, interest in the subject, comfort with ambiguity and willingness to take risk, to fail and learn from same.

Hence, the over-arching need to ask students "How did you approach this? How did you figure it out?" Their thinking is then shared with classmates so we can all learn from novel, effective and productive ways of analyzing and solving problems—not merely searching for the formula, plugging in values and doing the calculations.

Application

A. Identifying and resolving complex problems is what we do in all subjects.

Science/Technology: Figure out a way or ways to stop ocean pollution; spread of bacteria within a community center; create a process for measuring body mass in outer space . . .

Math: Given a specific lot within the community figure out the best/most economical use of 4" × 4" mosaic tiles to cover this irregular space. Given statistics on the city's Stop and Frisk policy (how many stopped, frisked, and for what publicly stated reasons), ask researchable questions and figure out how to answer each. (Actual assignment, Laura Mourino, Chapter Nine)

Art: Design the interior of a given school/community space to reflect the goals, vision and mission of the school. Use methods and major concepts of advanced art classes.

PE: Design a fitness program that meets the nutritional needs of a diverse school population in accordance with recent FDA and other AMA guidelines.

History: Identify a significant problem within any African (or other) nation. Pose questions, conduct research and develop a plan to remediate this problem. Be prepared to defend your proposed solutions to peers and experts.

B. Develop ways for students to record their problematic statement, their research questions; investigative processes and all other reflections on what they're learning. These might be written in paper notebooks, on Google Drive or any other electronic notepads–daily! If, like Tim, you can access these writings rather immediately, you will be able to monitor students' progress, provide timely feedback and guide them toward success.

C. Provide opportunities for students to share their findings with peers on several occasions so they can receive direct, meaningful feedback and make important modifications as necessary.

Appendix: STEM Goals and Criteria, Sandusky, OH

Presentational Skills

1. To improve presentation and communication skills. Students will be able to present using multi-media, group and individual presentation skills. Long term goal is Sr. Exit project.
   Communicate clearly:

Articulate thoughts and ideas effectively using oral, written and non-verbal communication skills in a variety of forms and contexts.

Listen effectively to decipher meaning, including knowledge, values, attitudes and intentions.

Use communication for a range of purposes (e.g. to inform, instruct, motivate and persuade).

Utilize multiple media and technologies, and know how to judge their effectiveness a priori as well as assess their impact.

Communicate effectively in diverse environments (including multi-lingual).

Creative and Innovative Thinking

2. To foster students' creativity and innovation. Students will use the district-wide design cycle to answer problems. Long term—encourage design cycle. (Obie)

Think Creatively:

Use a wide range of idea creation techniques (such as brainstorming).

Create new and worthwhile ideas (both incremental and radical concepts).

Elaborate, refine, analyze and evaluate their own ideas in order to improve and maximize creative efforts.

Work Creatively with Others:

Develop, implement and communicate new ideas to others effectively.

Be open and responsive to new and diverse perspectives; incorporate group input and feedback into the work.

Demonstrate originality and inventiveness in work and understand the real-world limits to adopting new ideas.

View failure as an opportunity to learn; understand that creativity and innovation is a long-term, cyclical process of small successes and frequent mistakes. (Emphasis added.)

Implement Innovations:

Act on creative ideas to make a tangible and useful contribution to the field in which the innovation will occur.

Group Collaboration

3. We will have students work in groups and learn to collaborate with other students and teachers. Long term—students will learn how to successfully

manage a large project and use contracts to hold people accountable. STEM Project and ICs.

Collaborate with Others:

Demonstrate ability to work effectively and respectfully with diverse teams.

Exercise flexibility and willingness to be helpful in making necessary compromises to accomplish a common goal.

Assume shared responsibility for collaborative work, and value the individual contributions made by each team member.

Think Critically and Solve Problems

4. To have students critically think. Research methods and proper citation. Students should be able to write an effective paper, with proper sources and work on MLA citation in all classes.

Reason Effectively:

Use various types of reasoning (inductive, deductive, etc.) as appropriate to the situation.

Use Systems Thinking:

Analyze how parts of a whole interact with each other to produce overall outcomes in complex systems.

Make Judgments and Decisions:

Effectively analyze and evaluate evidence, arguments, claims and beliefs.

Analyze and evaluate major alternative points of view.

Synthesize and make connections between information and arguments.

Interpret information and draw conclusions based on the best analysis.

Reflect critically on learning experiences and processes.

Solve Problems:

Solve different kinds of non-familiar problems in both conventional and innovative ways.

Identify and ask significant questions that clarify various points of view and lead to better solutions.

Chapter 9

Playgrounds of the Mind

The nature of problem solving

The car won't start . . .
The outdoor basketball facilities in your town are in very poor
shape . . .
Apple failed to reach its sales targets for the quarter . . .
And your spouse forgot your tenth wedding anniversary . . . !

These are all representations of different situations that didn't turn
out well.

They are all what we call "problems." That is, they tell us about unde-
sirable situations that need to be fixed, changed or otherwise improved, if
possible.

Here's a different set of situations:

Suppose that every hour of every day, an airplane leaves Los Angeles
for New York City and at the same instant, an airplane leaves New
York City for Los Angeles. Each flight takes 5 hours. In a single day,
how many airplanes originating in New York City will pass airplanes
originating in Los Angeles in the air?

If Mary sells five peaches in one day and ten the next day, what is
her percentage of sales growth?

Determine the fair market value of your Dream House to be
located within the five boroughs of New York City. Consider square
footage, amenities, location, maintenance and the like. Consult the
internet for key real estate data within your selected location. What
factors did you consider in deciding upon your type of mortgage?
Most challenging part of this experience? Justify and explain all
calculations in detail.

You, of course, recognize the latter three as examples of problems you
might have had to solve in a mathematics class. In fact, two of these were

used as learning experiences in Laura Mourino's Algebra 2 class. Laura's school, Harvest Collegiate, is a member of the New York Performance Standards Consortium, a group of schools exempt from State Regents exams (except ELA), because they have created rigorous, authentic intellectual challenges for students to engage and thereby demonstrate their readiness for college-level work.

One of these problems looks easier than the other two.

But each represents an intriguing situation to figure out. Students may have very different solutions to one of these problems; for others the solutions should be identical if calculations have been performed accurately.

Some problems, thus, are open ended with multiple possible answers— Apple sales and spousal forgetfulness. Some are closed, convergent with answers we can all agree upon.

In this way they are different from what we shall encounter later as examples of "critical thinking" judgments where we need to determine the truthfulness or believability of a claim such as "New Yorkers live longer." We shall explore this aspect of thinking more in Chapter Ten.

Definitions

What do we mean by the word "problem"?

The *Random House Dictionary of The English Language* says a problem is "Any question or matter involving doubt, uncertainty or difficulty." This closely parallels John Dewey's definition of thinking, that which commences with any question or issue involving "perplexity, hesitation [and/or] doubt." Dewey, (1910).

Interestingly, the etymology (derivation) of the word "problem" is from the Latin, Greek and Middle English, "obstacle . . . to lay before . . . [from *proballein*] to throw forward." This origin has always puzzled me, wondering what it meant to "lay before . . . throw forward." Perhaps it referred to a person's laying before a king, lord, magistrate, judge or person in authority a difficult situation—missing sheep or cattle—requiring future action.

Commonalities

What do the first set of four problems have in common with the latter set of three?

The problems with recreational facilities, financial markets, spousal relations and mechanics all invite our working toward some kind of solution, or not. We can ignore the personal relations issue if we dare. Apple will strive to improve. Basketball courts can be repaired or redesigned.

In each case, however, we have situations that invite investigation that might result in a variety of solutions, some acceptable, some not. There are decisions to be made and these will result in different qualities of solutions in accordance with our criteria.

With the mathematical problems, with one possible exception, each has a right or better answer. We will analyze the facts in the real estate market, seek out the important factors and come to conclusions and answers. Notice the important process is arriving at and justifying your reasonable conclusions.

With the airplane (LGA to LAX) and peaches problems, there will be convergent answers based upon non-disputable facts.

But what's common other than all seven reflect problems to solve?

1. They are characterized by "doubt, difficulty and uncertainty."

2. There isn't one definitive approach to a solution, even though with selling peaches, five peaches one day and ten the next there is a correct answer.

3. They require us to step back, analyze, using a variety of approaches toward resolution:

   a. Identify what's important, what's being asked for.

   b. Collect relevant facts.

   c. Represent, create a model.

   d. Break down into smaller parts.

   e. Consult resources for more information.

   f. Relate to similar problems already solved.

   g. Reflect on unstated and unsubstantiated assumptions.

   h. Formulate hypotheses or reasonable solutions.

4. They are not easily solved by using only "procedural math," that is, identifying a formula, plugging in the values and doing the calculations.

5. Each problem can result in an equally valid response if the response is authenticated or as this particular teacher stresses, "justified with evidence."

6. They each represent answers to the question "When will we ever use math?" by challenging students with real-world applications.

These are more "thought" than routine problems. All may be considered authentic, real-world problems, ones we might have to face one day.

They all can be analyzed using analytic approaches "a" through "h" above, all of which can be initiated as questions: "What's the problem and how might I approach it? Can I draw a picture, create a model? Can I solve a smaller part of the problem? How does this situation relate to others I might have encountered?" (Barell, 1995)

Problem analysis, therefore, involves our asking these kinds of questions in order to come to an understanding of what's involved and what we're being asked to do. It will mean, for example, disclosing hidden assumptions, that which is not stated.

This will be new for some students who, like me, have been used to identifying a formula and plugging in the numbers.

Here's what some of Laura's students wrote in their reflective journals about learning to solve problems:

> This math class is different from my other math classes because you don't tell us the answer to a problem right away. Rather, you would like us to think about it for a while so we can come up with the answer ourselves and fully understand how we got there. (Ashlyn)
>
> I am a visual learner, along with needing to talk out the problems I am doing. The easiest way for me to do my work is in groups, or with another person. (Sara)
>
> This class has taught me that it doesn't matter what strategy you use to get the sum of the problem, as long as you get the answer and are able to explain your reasoning, is what's important. (Rezarta)

Notice Ashlyn's comment: "You don't tell us the answer to a problem right away . . ." Must be that she's used to exactly this process. If students can't figure it out, the teacher often tells them the answer or makes it a lot easier to get that answer. This process makes students more dependant on us.

And what's really important, being able to "explain your reasoning."

Teaching Strategies

Teachers who engage students in this way often do the following:

1. Thinking aloud, modeling their own problem identification and resolution processes for students, even thinking through problems they have not yet seen.

2. Practicing in the following modes: individual, pairs and small groups.

3. Solving problems in pairs: one person articulates how she is thinking through the problem with a friend listening, checking for accuracy, pausing but not correcting. (Based on the Chicago University research of Benjamin Bloom (Bloom & Broder, 1950), an approach that elicited effective strategies such as representing in diagram or drawing, identifying key elements and approaching it in a systematic way.)

4. Writing in inquiry/problem-solving journals: "How I am solving this problem?" and "Reflections on what I'm learning about this process." Strong emphasis on "How did we solve this? What were our strategies?" and ample recognition that most problems have multiple approaches toward resolution.

5. Creating problems. Students create their own problems using basic ideas/concepts within the unit and exchange them for peers to solve.

6. Spending ample time on analytic approaches. This will involve the kinds of questions that need to be asked and mentioned above. Instead of asking, "OK, what's the problem and which formula do I use here?" we want to educate students to reflect on the kinds of questions they should be asking about identification, models, relationships and assumptions, thereby emphasizing their own personal control over the problem solving processes. One teacher of advanced math used to ask continually, "What questions do we need to ask about this/these problem/s?" We do not always seek to obtain the correct answer.

It's important to model for students how we go about analyzing problems, not merely remembering the appropriate formula and plugging in the values. (See the extensive research of Harold Stevenson, 1994, *The Learning Gap—Why our schools are failing and what we can learn from Japanese and Chinese schools* where he describes how teachers in some Asian countries follow this model: teach students how to analyze problems, not merely get the right answer. His research indicated that the latter approach was favored in US schools.)

One of the benefits of engaging in such problem solving, we ought to mention, was cited sixty years ago by an educational leader, Ralph Tyler in his *Basic Principles of Curriculum and Instruction*. Information, he said, can be efficiently acquired "at the same time that students are solving problems . . . When information is acquired as a part of problem solving, the use of the information and the reasons for obtaining it are clear. This is less likely to result in rote memorization" (1949, p. 73).

Figure 9.1

Analytic questions to ask about most problems, in math or other subjects:

Is this like any other problem I've seen?

How does it compare to other problems we've done?

How did we solve that problem?

Can I break it down into several parts? Solve each separately?

Can I represent/draw it out?

How can I reduce it to smaller parts?

What assumptions need to be identified/questioned?

Questions like those in Figure 9.1 can and should be asked about problems with numbers, with and about people and their relationships as well as about nature. Being able to analyze a problem, break it down into parts, challenge its assumptions, is more difficult than finding a formula into which to plug numbers, but then human problems don't often lend themselves to using formulae!

Challenges

A major challenge in problem-solving instruction is what I've referred to as "solve all the even-numbered problems, correct the homework and hand in." This approaches the mindlessness that may characterize problem-solving instruction, over-reliance on "procedural math" without the challenge to spend time on problem analysis. It's the "rote memorization" Tyler refers to above.

Here's where the analytic approaches above may come in to play: Represent, Reduce, Relate and so forth . . .

Another challenge is confronting the "three second rule." I first heard of this from teachers working with early elementary students. "If they cannot solve it in three seconds, the hands go up and they give up." I've seen the same phenomenon in high school math, in Laura Mourino's Algebra 2 class where some of her students came to her in that frame of mind. If they cannot figure it out in a very short period of time, they push the problem away and give up. She actively sought, through modeling and teaching good problem-solving processes, to help students "manage" their impulsive desire to say, "I can't do this" (Art Costa, 2012, personal communications).

Yet another challenge may be our reluctance to challenge students with problems they have not yet seen. "They won't know what to do!"

Overcoming this challenge requires thorough knowledge of what students already do know and our ability to instill confidence within them.

Willingness to jump into the unknown with "I'm not sure how you're going to go about this, but I know you have the required knowledge to analyze this problem and to figure out a solution. Use your iPhones if you need to," I heard Laura say as she presented problems like the real estate one mentioned above.

Other challenges to becoming better at problem solving including lacking significant background knowledge. This may involve inexperience as well as lack of a conceptual framework for analyzing. If students have absolutely no knowledge of air travel nor of urban real estate, they will be at a significant disadvantage.

And, finally, there will be problems that are conceptually too challenging. They demand a quality of abstract thinking students have not yet developed, that is, "Formal Operational" thinking as described by Jean Piaget. They will have difficulty with proportional reasoning ($a/b = c/d$; "How was Kaiser Wilhelm like Hitler?"). (See Chapter Three, "Developing Abstract Reasoning.")

Lastly, as Laura explained to me,

> Educators will often say, "it is too late" to teach them how to think this way. It is never too late, whether it is getting a student during their senior year, or wanting to revamp your curriculum in March. It simply requires a concerted effort on the educators' behalf to *persist* in providing these types of problem and be *constant* in demanding students to tackle these problems regularly until the students realize this is now part of the class expectation, it is not going away and their grade relies heavily on this so there is no other better choice on the student's behalf than to learn to persevere on the problems. (Personal communication, March, 2014)

As a final note, many educators will say these types of problems are not possible in an overbearing testing environment, especially when state and local standardized tests are just one of the many problematic tools used in evaluating students. Laura would argue that these tasks are far more enriching in preparing students exactly for the type of questions that appear on typical standardized assessments since all these tasks require multiple connections to past analytical skills. Consider, for instance, the peach problem which utilizes verbal problems that will require formulating an algebraic model that must be solved along with a decent number sense foundation.

Problem–Solving Playgrounds in Mathematics

As I mentioned above, two of the three more convergent problem situations presented at the opening of this chapter came from Laura Mourino's Algebra 2 class in New York City. Laura teaches at Harvest Collegiate High School on West Fourteenth Street. I spent one day a week in her class of high school juniors during the years 2013 to 2014 and less frequently in 2015. A multi-talented educator, Laura teaches all levels of high school math.

She is an educator whom I wish I had had in high school, because she regularly challenged her students with authentic, non-traditional, not-one-right-answer kinds of problematic situations, always giving them the confidence they could find excellent ways of solving same. "Use your iPads if you need to look up something," she'd say as students almost always worked in groups at their tables, collaborating and, occasionally, learning from students who became the local experts from different tables.

Hence, Laura sees her classroom as a mathematical "playground where we all make mistakes. There's no pressure . . . You're testing out your own hypotheses . . . ruling out and ruling in [approaches, solutions]," she'll tell her students as they struggle through problem identification and different ways of analyzing said problem. (Jacob Bronowski, physicist and poet, once observed "Discoveries are made by people who are constantly getting the wrong answer . . . Progress is the exploration of our own error," 1978, pp. 111–112.)

As I've mentioned above, Harvest Collegiate is part of the New York Performance Standards Consortium, meaning that Laura and others create their own benchmark tests for students (Figure 9.2) and do not, therefore, rely on somebody else's standardized-bubble-tests to assess students and, ultimately, themselves.

Benchmark Performances

Civic Planning

To get a good picture of overall change in one student's thinking over time, I will present an early assessment of her thinking.

Figure 9.2 Benchmark, Pre-Post Test Criteria for Assessment

LEARNING GOAL:

Problem Solving:

I use my own creative thoughts and examples to develop appropriate, thoughtful, and efficient strategies to find solutions to problems.

Reasoning and Proof:

I support my observations and claims with multiple forms of appropriate mathematical evidence to support these assertions.

Communications:

I communicate my mathematical ideas clearly in multiple ways.

Representation:

I create appropriate models, inherent to the task, that represent the problem accurately and elegantly.

Connections:

I can discuss how mathematical concepts interconnect and build upon each other. I apply concepts to real-world situations.

[Please note the criterion Reasoning and Proof, because we will encounter virtually the same language in Chapter Eleven when discussing reasoning in Physics 1 and another social studies class entitled Looking for an Argument: Basing Conclusions upon Reasons, and Evidence. The essence of mathematical as well as humanities-types of thinking is drawing conclusions based upon appropriate, representative, accurate evidence.]

In February 2013, before I entered Laura's classroom in the fall of that year, Laura challenged her students to figure out an appropriate number of facilities required to serve the needs of a population of 100,000 people within four boroughs in Harvest City: to include hospitals, public schools and colleges; police and fire; religious centers, movie theaters, malls, restaurants, McDonald's, Starbuck's and Day Care centers.

Wilette was given demographic data (how many residents under 5, 5–17 and so forth up to 65+) as well as twelve different internet sites of census, demographic, urban planning, home design, land use and population growth data.

Laura's charge:

> Explain your analytic approach in determining the number of facilities you identified for a population base of 100,000. Please be sure to *provide a clear mathematic justification* as to how you derived your responses . . . Make sure your analysis includes efficient and appropriate *mathematic reasoning* as well as any and all formulas, diagrams/representations, etc. in providing your justification."
> (Emphasis added)

Wilette's responses:

> The way that I figured out the right amount of facilities and how many people they would service is by first looking at all our NYC's boroughs, looking up all the hospitals, schools, malls, restaurants and etc. And once I got a general sense of how many of these things I would need to have in my city I started to put in numbers in the columns [provided in the problem] and when I finished I would picture all the facilities and I realized that I had put in too many facilities and it would not make any sense so I shrunk the number pictured it in my head until I saw the right amount of these facilities in my city so that it wouldn't look like no one lived there cause I also had to take into account that I needed room for the building and house for the people who would live there.
>
> The way that I chose 6 to be the right number for the hospitals because I feel like we wouldn't need more than that amount, also 2 of those hospitals could be used as specialty hospitals like for cancer or just a children's hospital . . . I chose 24 ambulances that way each hospital could have 4 ambulances for themselves . . .

At first Wilette thought she'd have the same number (unspecified) of elementary, middle and high schools, but then reasoned that "many kids don't go through with high school because they have to help their family or they just don't feel like they need to go to school anymore . . ."

She continued with colleges: "The reason why I have very few universities and colleges is because many people don't really go to college so it wouldn't make sense to me to make 20–25 colleges that won't be educating anyone . . ."

She reasoned that there ought to be one religious building for each group; she settled on seven total.

And

> The way I figured out how many people would come to these facilities in one year was by thinking about a reasonable number of about how many people would come to them and writing it down. The way that I figured out what that number would be in 10 years [also a requirement] was by multiplying that number by 10.

Reflective Pause

Without knowing at this point how Laura scored Wilette's reasoning through this city design and construction problem, take a moment to reflect on your own analysis in accordance with the criteria in Figure 9.2. What do you like? What tentative conclusions might you draw about her mathematical reasoning? Why? What questions would you have asked Wilette about her thinking? Why?

Laura's Reflections

Problem Solving—*Student is truly thinking deeply about the problem and started by using the local community as the starting point of reference to make connection to the broader problem at hand. Student takes into account aesthetic constraints factors as a determinant of the number of facilities. Student begins to focus on specifics of the problem when she identifies the types of hospitals that would be needed, which was not asked in the original problem.*

However, student does not utilize classroom experiences to the problem at hand as she does not relate this as an extension of several existing analytical approaches done in class to determine quantitatively the number for these facilities. There is no true analytical problem solving approach but rather a generalized extension of her colloquial experiences to answer this problem and she does not begin to approximate/generalize long-term consequences of her choice such as population growth and urban sprawl.

GRADE 1.5

Evidence—*The only evidence the student gave was based on her colloquial experiences which are insufficient to come to a clear conclusion.*
GRADE 1

Communication—(Student will not be graded on grammar or ELA structure. Related concerns will be personally addressed with student and her ELA instructor.) *Student has clearly indicated how her response was obtained. I still have to infer quite a bit as to the specific identification of each number of facilities. It is unclear why she chose to use this strategy over others, including using already existing models derived in class. It is also unclear how she determined the specific number of hospitals, etc.*
GRADE 2

Second Benchmark, September 2013

Now, here's the problem Laura used as a benchmark for students' progress in September:

> Sue Flay opened a McDonald's on White Plains Road and Cassa Role opened a Burger King across the street. Both had to borrow money to open their fast food franchises. After 500 customers, Sue was still $4,000 in debt. By the time she had served 3,000 customers, she was ahead $1,000.
>
> After 2,000 customers, Cassa Role still owed $6,000 to the bank. However, after 45 customers, she was ahead by $1,500.
>
> Which restaurant would you rather own? (Hint: At what points do you want to own them?)

In working out this problem Wilette used arithmetic calculations: $500 + 300 = 800$; $4,000 - 1,000 = 3,000$.

She mapped out a solution using a columnar table, one for Day One at McDonald's and one for Day One at Burger King:

McDonald's	Burger King
Day 1 owes $4,000	Day 1 owes $6,000
Customers 3,000	Customers 4,500
Made $1,000	Made $1,500
Now owes $3,000	Now owes $4,500
Day 2 3,000 more customers	Day 2 4,500 more customers
Made $1,000	Made $1,500
Owes $2,000	Owes $3,000

And on to Days 3 and 4 with similar logic.
Wilette concludes:

I would rather own Burger King because even though they were out of debt the same day as McDonald's, they get more customers than McD's. The amount of customers McD's needed to break even was 9,000 customers . . . [for Burger King] was 13,500.

Reflective Pause

Examine Wilette's approach to the hamburger problem: What is she doing here that was absent from her reasoning in the Harvest City problem six months prior? How has her thinking grown/developed in that time?

Laura's Reflections

In comparison to her previous task, Wilette has made a huge jump in starting to formulate quantitative models to generalize this situation. She is thinking deeply but with a more quantitative and analytical mind and now knows that I am demanding a response that will involve a more scientific approach. Her responses are no longer based on past experiences but rather on her in-class experiences coupled with a more scientific approach of quantifying her response. Wilette could have expanded her thinking by providing a "second approach" such as graphing the situation to check if she is on right track. Technically, the problem never suggests that the goal is to have a company with high profits but simply asks which do you prefer. And in Wilette's case, she clearly prioritizes having more customers above all. To that end, she has provided valid and sufficient evidence to indicate that Burger King will have more customers. Not clear if Wilette understands at what expense these extra customers will come by. In terms of communication, while she is now able to justify her response quantitatively, I still have to infer quite a bit as to why she chose this particular strategy.

    Problem solving: 2.5
    Evidence: 3
    Communication: 2.5

Third Benchmark December 2013

Three months later (December, 2013) Laura administered a third benchmark. See how or if Wilette's mathematical reasoning has matured in that time:

> The problem: Suppose that every hour of every day, an airplane leaves Los Angeles for New York City and at the same instant, an airplane leaves New York City for LA. Each flight takes 5 hours. In a single day, how many airplanes originating in NYC will pass airplanes originating in LA in the air?

Now, Wilette's response paper has three forms of reasoning: A diagram/picture; a table of landings and take-offs and a written description.

Picture

Where they meet in the air

NY _____ 5 Hr Period _____ LA

Table

```
1 am NY left @ 1am        arrive @ 6 am
LA left @ 1 am            arrive 6 am
2 am NY @ 2 am            Arrive @ 7 am
LA @ 2 am                 Arrive @ 7 am
And so on from 1 am to 12 am
```

Written Description of Wilette's Reasoning

> There will be a total of 24 airplanes that pass each other because as it states "Every hour of every day" an airplane from LA and an airplane from NY leaves. [Each takes five hours to make the cross-country journey.] So since it takes them the same amount of time to reach their destination and since they both leave every hour they will always be in the air at the same time. So because they leave every hour and there are 24 hours in one day there will be a total of 24 airplanes.

Reflective Pause

What changes in Wilette's mathematical reasoning do you see from April through September to December, 2013? Please see the end of the chapter for my analysis of Wilette's thinking.

Has she grown to become more able to analyze thoroughly, and draw reasoned conclusions that are less reliant upon her feelings of what ought to be?

Conclusion

Laura's examples stem from authentic, real-world problems, ones that are open to multiple entry approaches or strategies. Once again Ralph Tyler noted: "It is also desirable that the problems be set up in the kind of environment in which such problems usually arise in life" (1949, p. 69). In other words, where they are "authentic."

Different students approached them in various ways.

This is what makes teaching subjects like math (and others) so exciting: we never know exactly how students will use their prior knowledge and mathematical reasoning abilities to analyze and solve a problem. Hence, it's sometimes important to focus only upon approaches, upon the analysis process of problem solving as mentioned above.

Mathematical reasoning *is* the content of this course. (See Chapter Two, "Curricular Framework for Authentic Learning and Assessment.")

A major difference between problem solving in math and social studies is that the former is almost always considered to result in convergent, right/ wrong answers. This is not, however, how students in Laura's classroom learned algebra, trigonometry, calculus and statistics.

What I loved about Laura's math classes was her willingness to put forth very rigorous and intellectually challenging problematic scenarios for students—some involving dinosaur digs, a police policy here in New York called "Stop and Frisk" and ones involving establishing businesses—and then gave her students ample time to play with them, meaning sufficient opportunities to try, to fail and try again, to follow their hunches, to mess about with all the important elements.

Yes, some, a very few, would give up within three minutes. I saw one young man sprawl upon his work table, saying with his body prone toward the ceiling, "I can't *do* this, Laura."

"Yes, you can. Keep at it," she responded lovingly, perhaps providing a clue as she passed by his table.

By the end of the class this very student was rushing about the room showing his mates how to do it! He'd figured it out.

Perhaps he, like Nobel-prize-winning physicist Richard Feynman, used his body to help him think, to imagine, to take different approaches to situations.

Application: My Analysis of Wilette's Thinking

1. How does Wilette "develop appropriate, thoughtful and efficient strategies" to solve each of these problems?

2. In a workshop recently, one participant noted that Laura's benchmarks were "not typical math assignments." Do you agree/disagree? Why? What if you'd had a teacher like Laura?

3. What elements—levels of intellectual challenge, nature of authenticity within problem, personal choices—can you adapt to your own classroom?

4. To what extent do you engage in performance assessments like these? How would you use a benchmark like one of these in a future unit?

Develop a Community

Wilette follows a step-by-step process: "by first looking at all the boroughs [in NYC]."

She conducted Research on a real area to determine what its facilities were, to serve as a model, a Representation.

Then she visualized what she had, another internal representation.

Reasoning that initial solutions were too large, she reduced the number of facilities, schools, hospitals, etc. How did she reach this conclusion? What assumptions was she making? Or was she comparing facilities in the model with her own and making adjustments? In part, she used her prior knowledge, "Many kids don't go through high school . . ." with which to make adjustments.

Use of Reasoning and Proof: I would give her a "Proficient" (not "expert") because the reader has to "infer what I am trying to argue and validate," say for example, with the number of people who visit a facility. I was intrigued by her use there of visualizations: "I shrunk the number pictured it in my head until I saw the right amount of these facilities in my city . . ." Based upon what assumptions, prior knowledge?

Notice how she determined the number of hospitals: "because I feel . . ." She may be right, but such a feeling is different from basing her decision upon comparative data, for example.

Thus, she shows clear approaches, but ones only sometimes based upon good mathematical reasoning, e.g. comparing her draft with a model. There are too many unstated assumptions leading to mathematical conclusions.

Establishing a Business

Wilette breaks the problem into two logical parts.

She represents each part with data relating to sales and reduction of debt, starting with Day 1 and proceeding forward

Use of Reasoning and Proof: She uses mathematical data to arrive at a choice, a preference for Burger King because of the greater number of customers. She assumes greater sales, therefore. Good assumption?

Cross-continental Air Flights

With respect to problem-solving strategies, here's what I see.

She again uses a step-by-step approach.

She Reduces the problem down to smaller parts, creating a visual Representation/picture for each flight's taking off and landing during the twenty-four hour period.

Use of Reasoning and Proof: Wilette uses the evidence supplied in the problem statement to arrive at her answer, twenty-four planes from New York City will pass planes originating from Los Angeles. Her breaking the problem into small units and representing each part with a mathematical model, helps her reason toward this correct solution.

What seems to be the essence of her growth in mathematical reasoning is her becoming far more comfortable with three different kinds of representations (the airplane and franchise problems) and leaving behind a kind of imagining/guesswork/feeling approach without hard data in the Harvest City problem.

No one uses the same processes, but Figure 9.3 shows research-based approaches that can help us analyze complex situations.

Figure 9.3

> Problem-solving processes Wilette used:
>
> Reducing it to smaller parts
>
> Representing the problem in different ways
>
> Conducting research
>
> Reflecting on assumptions
>
> Comparing to similar problems
>
> Following a step-by-step process
>
> Using prior/background knowledge
>
> Drawing conclusions based on evidence.

Vizualization can be considered a kind of internal representation and we know how important such was for the radical thinking of Einstein, who said, "I think in more or less clear images . . ." So, Wilette's picturing to solve a problem has grown from having an image in her mind to using such pictures in the airplane problem to arrive at better solutions.

In all three problems she used a step-by-step process to arrive at a solution. She commenced her Harvest City problem thusly:

> By *first* looking at all our boroughs [in NYC], looking up all the hospitals, schools, malls, restaurants . . . And once I got a general sense of how many of these things I would need . . . I started to put *numbers in the columns* [for same] and when I finished *I would picture* all the facilities and I realized that I had put too many facilities and it would not make any sense so I shrunk the number *pictured it in my head* until I saw the right amount . . . (Emphases added)

Perhaps an over-reliance on internal imagery?

On the other hand, she used common sense and knowledge of current educational practices (not all kids go to college) to figure out the number of institutions of higher learning. One other student reasoned: "The schools such as elementary, middle and high schools are near each other because it has to do with education . . . The colleges and universities are near the garden because students can learn about Horticulture and other related programs."

In all three problems she does indeed break them down into smaller parts or units: proceeding to establish numbers of schools, police/fire stations, apartment buildings (as did other students). In the hamburger problem she took it day-by-day. Unfortunately, her understanding of how many daily customers there were may have led to incorrect calculations, but in the airplane problem she plotted out all of the various parts and that led her to a better, correct answer.

Finally, she was the only student among those I followed more closely who, in the city design problem, practiced the key problem-solving process of conducting Research—looking at all the other boroughs to establish solid benchmarks for her own internal image of a good city design. She compared these benchmarks with her initial, tentative calculations and decided that her results were unacceptable. Comparing one's own ideas and solutions with data and/or with others' ideas is a most powerful way of reasoning— use of "appropriate mathematical evidence to support assertions."

References

Barell, J. (1995) *Teaching for Thoughtfulness—Classroom strategies to enhance intellectual development* (2nd edn). New York: Longman.

Bloom, B.S., & Broder, L. (1950) *The Problem Solving Processes of College Students*. Chicago: University of Chicago Press.

Bronowski, J. (1978) *The Origins of Knowledge and Imagination*. New Haven: Yale University Press.

Dewey, J. (1910) *How We Think*. Boston: D.C. Heath.

Stevenson, H. (1994) *The Learning Gap—Why our schools are failing and what we can learn from Japanese and Chinese schools*. New York: Simon & Schuster.

Tyler, R. (1949) *Basic Principles of Curriculum and Instruction*. Chicago: University of Chicago Press.

Chapter 10

Critical Thinking about Social Issues

Recurrent Rhythms

In both Chapters Ten and Eleven we will be dealing with what we call "critical thinking," defined as the willingness and ability to draw reasoned conclusions, or claims, based upon relevant, representative and verifiable evidence.

We engage in this kind of thinking in every discipline and area of life and it is important to delve deeply into thinking with the predisposition for reasoned judgment. As we shall see, there is far too much undisciplined thinking today, especially in these days of 24/7 media coverage of events. Early "claims" about terrible events often turn out to be untrue. Truth requires the patient, persistent pursuit of all the evidence in order to draw these reasoned conclusions.

In every subject we teach, we are encouraging students to make such reasoned judgments or claims, not merely in social studies and science.

Old Wives' Tales

People used to say: "Eating too much chocolate leads to acne." "Consuming ice cream causes nightmares."

They also used to think that opening an umbrella indoors led to bad luck.

These are examples of what we now call "old wives' tales," stories swapped by women, and probably men, to be instructive, to prevent bad habits.

Evidence to support any one of these? Doesn't exist.

Totally unfounded by contemporary science and, mostly, ignored today except for humor.

Our popular culture abounds in statements, some of which may be unfounded:

"We never landed on the moon . . ."

"School choice leads to higher students' achievement . . ."

"Put a tooth in a bottle of Coke and it will disappear overnight . . ."

"Cutting taxes spurs economic growth . . ."

Evidence for Our Claims and Conclusions

Today we have examples of thinking where our conclusions are based upon fact.

Some people affirm that "The planet is warming . . . Use ample amounts of sun screen on your skin lest you suffer from various cancers later in life."

For these claims there is evidence, solid, concrete, verifiable data.

The difference between an "old wives' tale" and an assertion about climatology is that the latter can be supported with real data, evidence from thousands of observers, whereas the former cannot. Whether or not you choose to use sun screen is, of course, a matter of personal choice, but there is confirming evidence to support what doctors are telling us.

Critical thinking is the use of our intelligent faculties in order to establish the value or worth of a claim, conclusion or proposed course of action.

We use the word "claim" here to refer to a reasoned judgment, one achieved after considering evidence and, therefore, different qualitatively from an "opinion." People often say, "Well, my opinion is as good as anybody else's." True, especially when this involves your preference for coffee ice cream, the movie *The Hunger Games*, the Boston Celtics or New York Yankees.

But as a distinguished and late New York Senator, Daniel Patrick Moynihan, once observed, "Everyone is entitled to his own opinion, but not to his own facts." Claims need to be supported by facts, facts that are verifiable by all, not just in science, but in all of human affairs.

Virtually every school district's philosophy aims to develop students who are good, responsible citizens. This, at a minimum, entails being able to analyze complex issues, gather information and draw reasoned conclusions, ones that would help solve pressing problems.

Recall the "Vision of the Graduate" from Greenwich, CT. They want students to "pose and pursue substantive questions" and next to be able to "critically interpret, evaluate, and synthesize information."

A responsibility for all citizens unless we wish to wallow in shared ignorances.

Definitions of Critical Thinking

There are several good definitions of critical thinking that I have used over the years:

♦ John McPeck (1981): critical thinking involves "a certain skepticism or suspension of assent toward a given statement, established norm, or mode of doing things." (p. 6)

♦ Matthew Lipman defined critical thinking as reflective thinking that is concerned with criteria, sensitive to context and self-correcting. (Personal communication, 1988)

♦ Harvey Siegel defined critical thinking as "Thinking appropriately moved by reasons." (Sawaya, 2012)

♦ And Robert Ennis (2011) defined it as "rational, reflective thinking concerned with what to do or believe . . ."

So, what do we see amongst these different definitions? Looking at them now for the first time together in several years, I'm struck by their similarities:

Critical thinking involves giving reasons, presumably good reasons, for what to do, say or believe.

In order to arrive at such conclusions we might be exercising due skepticism about various claims or judgments, e.g. "Smaller government is better," or "We should spend our way out of recession."

It is Matt Lipman's definition of critical thinking as employing criteria that is often overlooked. What Dr. Lipman, a former colleague at the Institute for Critical Thinking at Montclair State University, meant is that when we make a judgment about a good book, film, baseball team, learning experience or presidency we are using criteria. These are our reasons.

For example, to claim that *Gone with the Wind* was the best film ever made requires that we have certain criteria or reasons for making this judgment: plot, story, setting, actors, themes, quality of direction and so forth. And, of course, we need to be able to give specific information about the performances, for example, of Clark Gable, Vivien Leigh and others to support our reasons.

So, whenever one of our students says, "This is the best/worst book I ever read!" we can just calmly respond with "Oh, really. For what reasons? Why do you say that?"

Common Core State Standards/NGSS

So, in the Common Core State Standards (CCSS), children in First Grade are being challenged to "Ask and answer questions about key details in a text." Why? So they can form a judgment about the characters and the plot, for one reason. John Selkirk teaches Grade One in the Ottawa-Carlton school district and he challenges his students to be able to use context clues to support their ideas, for example about whether or not the characters appear happy or sad. "You can say what you want, but you have to give a reason for saying it" (Barell, 2012, p. 79). Imagine developing this responsibility so young!

By Third Grade the CCSS states, students will "Ask and answer questions to demonstrate understanding of a text, referring explicitly to the text as the basis for the answers," that is, giving good reasons with supportive data.

Since we will be discussing reasoning in science in Chapter Eleven, here's what the Next Generation Science Standards calls a "Crosscutting concept: Simple tests can be designed to gather evidence to support or refute student ideas about causes. (K-PS2–1), (K-PS2–2)" It was when attending a summer workshop of physics teachers at Teachers College, Columbia University in the summer of 2013 that I first heard one say, "This is my claim and here are my reasons."

And, as Andy and Steve reminded me on several occasions, the C3 Social Studies Standards focus upon an "Inquiry Arc" reflected in both their classes. The framework emphasizes "developing questions and planning inquiries" requiring the use of disciplinary tools and concepts (C3 Standards, n.d., 20, pp. 6, 12).

Thus, from humanities to sciences, those two worlds some see as disparate but others[1] have seen as grounded firmly in similar mental operations like imaginative thinking, we have a search for understandings that rely on good information, data and evidence.

Recurring Riffs

In music a "riff" is a short, repeated phrase often played over changing chords. The "riffs" we speak of here relate to being a good critical thinker.

When we confront some problematic situations—be they thorny issues of health care within our communities or figuring out maximum trajectories for projectiles—we will need to *think* first before we draw conclusions supported by evidence. What does this mean? Here we can use John McPeck's definition of critical thinking, that is, "a certain skepticism" that will lead to asking good, tough questions about problems.

For example,

What is the problem? (Identify. The most difficult question to answer with complex human issues. Our problem statement determines our solutions and whether or not we actually solve it.)

How to describe it? Major characters or elements? (Reduce to parts.)

What causes this issue? (Seek causal elements.)

What are we assuming to be true about it? (Reflect on assumptions.)

How might it be related to other similar ones? (Notice similarities/differences.)

What resources do I need to understand this situation?

And, what questions are still unanswered that I need to research?

Once we have some answers and conducted some research, we might be ready to form tentative conclusions about taking a position or favoring a solution.

Critical thinking, then, involves doing hard analytic thinking—often posing probing questions—before we are ready to cite our Conclusions with Reasons and Evidence. In Chapter Eleven Mike Zitolo calls these "pushing questions."

With our definitions and the core elements we can identify the key elements to be used as a guide for instruction and for assessment of students' thinking abilities. Commonly called a rubric, scoring guide, Likert scale, these sets of significant elements reflect our instructional priorities, concerns and goals. (See Figure 10.1)

Instructional Approaches

Foundational for this book is the idea that we foster students' intellectual growth and development by engaging them in considering and thinking through complex, authentic problematic situations, ones not easily resolved with simple solutions.

How do we foster such complex thinking in our classrooms?

There are so many fascinating ways to challenge students to think, draw conclusions and give good reasons. Here are a few.

A. John Selkirk's approach: look at pictures, passages in literature, videos and answer questions such as "What are the characters thinking? How do we know?" This First Grade example is replicable on up the ladder to high school and beyond: examine evidence and draw conclusions.

B. Presenting complex issues, at high school level, to think through and draw conclusions about such as those Andy Snyder (see below) used with his Argumentation class: anti-crime programs ("Stop and Frisk" in NYC); ethical dilemmas involving acquisition of high technologies; international crises (Afghanistan/Crimea/Middle East); health care and the like. Analyze, ask some of the questions above and conduct research before making a judgment.

C. Being book, film or drama critics wherein students make judgments about artists' craft and give good reasons. Write a title for a passage or chapter or a painting.

D. Playing Devil's Advocate, presenting reasons/evidence contrary to others' points of view . . . "Harry Truman/Ronald Reagan was a good president/leader." "Hitler was a bad leader." You might hear people in reasoned discussions say, "Just to play Devil's Advocate here . . ." and challenge the group to look at contrary evidence that does not support the prevailing common wisdom.

E. Playing a game known as "Philosophical Chairs," where students take one position, present/argue merits, debate and then switch, presenting the other side.

Critical Thinking in the Classroom

During the course of three years working with the high school teachers presented in this volume I have witnessed all of the definitions given above at play in one form or another.

Our task now is to illustrate just how critical thinking plays a role. We will start with identifying what one teacher, Andy Snyder of Harvest Collegiate High School on West Fourteenth Street, Manhattan, has done in his class.[2]

Figure 10.1 illustrates the kind of framework or rubric we can create for assessing students' critical thinking abilities.

What do you notice about each criterion and the wording of different levels of achievement?

For example, with respect to claims, we're looking for ones that are "precise, sound." In terms of reasons we want those that see the complexity of various problematic situations like what to do about immigration policies. Knowing how Andy Snyder and his colleague Stephen Lazar taught this class on argumentation, I know they were seeking claims that were more than "precise, sound." They wanted ones that reflected the complexity of the given situation, and were not simplistic. The complexity probably was

Figure 10.1 Harvest/Collegiate Social Studies Benchmark Writing Rubric

Learning Goal	Exceeds Goal	Meets Goal	Approaches Goal
Claim/Reasons	Establishes/develops a precise, sound claim and its significance, with coherent, complex supporting reasons		
Counter Claim	**Fairly** develops and integrates or refutes counter claim including **cited evidence** for reasons		
Selection of Evidence	Most **relevant, accurate verifiable,** convincing evidence for reasons		
Use of Evidence	**Thoroughly** explains how evidence supports each claim		
	Integrates evidence to maintain flow of ideas, **avoiding over-reliance** on any one source		
Organization	Orders claims, reasons/evidence across paragraphs and uses transitional words to clarify reasoning . . .		
Connections	Paper shows a **somewhat informed** awareness of how claims fit and relate to the larger context		
	Provides a **basic** answer to the question, "So what?" by exploring broader implications of argument		

more evident in the reasons and evidence given to support their positions. One of the goals of each of these educators was, indeed, to help their students understand that these issues are complex and not given to simplistic, "bumper-sticker mentality" or overtly politically motivated solutions.

In terms of evidence we sift that through the lens of that which is "relevant, accurate and verifiable." Excellent criteria for all evidence. I would add the word "reliable" to this list. Who are our reliable sources of information, more free from bias than others?

Figure 10.1 gives some of the priorities established by the Harvest team consisting of Stephen Lazar, Andy Snyder and others.

I have intentionally left portions of this rubric blank so you could work on them yourself. Once you have figured out what reflects *outstanding* performance, I've found, it is not that difficult to flesh out the rest. The criteria and contents will, of course, reflect your own priorities for students' achievement.

Assessments/Problematic Scenarios

Andy Snyder's approach was to present his students with what I've called earlier (Chapter Two) authentic learning challenges in the form of problematic scenarios that often require them to make a decision about what to do or say, such as New York City's anti-crime program "Stop and Frisk" or the federal government's food stamp program. Should we cancel one and cut the other?

These challenges or problematic scenarios are characterized by:

Complexity—of ideas, issues.

Multi-faceted in terms of approaches to understand, solve.

Interdisciplinarity of concepts.

Reflection of major ideas/concepts/skills/dispositions within units.

Requirement to think productively, critically, solving problems, creating works of art, hypothesizing, testing and evaluating.

How does he create such a problematic situation or scenario?

1. Select current, topical, significant issues of interest to students.
2. Identify a portion thereof within which one can solve a problem or make a decision.

3. Provide enough background knowledge for context.

4. Ensure academic rigor, active engagement, authenticity and opportunities to take alternative courses of action.

(based on Gallavan, 2009, p. 123)

Recent (2011) research with younger students indicates that when we encourage students to deal with conflicts, controversies and problems while studying topics like strip mining or endangered species they learn the material better (Engel, 2011, p. 628). [3] Why do you think this might be so?

This makes perfect sense, because the more we engage students in significant intellectual processes, problem solving, decision making, comparing/contrasting, explaining those Level II processes of the Three Story Intellect (Figure 5.1), the more they will retain what they are thinking about.

Instructional Framework

Andy's instructional framework called for him to spend a week on each topic in a regular departmental course called "Looking for an Argument," during which he taught students how to write:

Claims/Conclusions
  with Good Reasons
    Supported by Evidence

And then, he added making Counter Claims with Evidence and determining Warrants justifying uses of evidence.

What made this class unique in my experience was a strategy involving debates between Andy Snyder and his colleague Stephen Lazar at the introduction of a topic. One would advocate for terminating Stop and Frisk, citing some carefully selected studies, and then the other would counter that with his own set of data. Students would listen, take notes and then ask each other questions after the teachers posed questions of each other. Seeing adults debate an issue is not what high school students are used to and this was often enlivening and spirited. Obviously, Andy and Steve would select data to support their point of view and, occasionally, would present some not-too-reputable nor reliable source to challenge their ability to ask questions about reliability of sources.[4]

In general their week proceeded thusly:

Monday: Open debate with questions from students.

Tuesday–Wednesday: Researching topic.

Thursday: Rough draft writing.

Friday: Final essay with Claims, Reasons and Evidence (plus, later in semester, Counter Claims, Reasons and Evidence).

Justin's Critical Thinking

Justin is a student who came to Harvest Collegiate "with what appeared at the time to be lower skills and lower motivation" and Andy shared his work with me (with permission as in all cases of students' work).

The first benchmark challenge involved a personal scenario:

> Your friend advises that he has just stolen two brand new iPhone 5s and wants to give you one since he knows you really wanted it and your parents won't get you one. Your friend refuses to let you know where he got them, but assures you there is no chance the phones will be tracked. What would you do?

Here is Justin's response:

> If your friend offered you a highly-valued stolen good, you shouldn't take it. Stealing is wrong to begin with and by taking something your friend stole, you're aiding a crime. Even if your friend assures you they can't be traced, the police might find another way to trace the phone to you. If you wait and your parents buy it for you, you'll feel better inside and the experience will be more enjoyable.

 ## Reflective Pause

This is Justin's entire response. Others wrote two and three times as much as did Justin.

Now, using the criteria in Figure 10.1, how would you assess Justin's performance on this first writing challenge? Claim, Counter Claim, Evidence?

Andy Snyder's Analysis

Here's how Andy analyzed Justin's thinking in this initial benchmark:

> *What's Justin done? He's inhabited the imaginary situation and provided a meaningful and clear response to what he would do and why. He's*

provided two reasons—the moral injunction against stealing and the practical likelihood of punishment. This demonstrates a real strength of many of my students these days—the ability to make a straightforward statement of their own opinion. We also see a bit of counter-claim—his friend says the phone won't be traceable but Justin realizes that other means of tracking the phone (unknown to his friend) might be available to the police (this unit preceded Edward Snowden's revelations of the NSA's iPhone hacking). And we see some imagination—he fantasizes his likely emotions if he refused this phone but received an unstolen one from his parents.

What's Justin not done? Justin hasn't provided an analysis of whether he should turn his friend in. He hasn't developed any of his starting assumptions (about theft, the worth of iPhones, his relationship with his friend).

What do you think of Justin's use of "Relevant, Accurate, Verifiable" evidence?

You be the judge.

Notice Andy's assertion that Justin has "inhabited the imaginary situation," using his own imagination. Recall in Chapter Five our discussion of the many, varied ways we do challenge students to think imaginatively. Justin's challenge was a moral dilemma, steal or not. It requires that you think yourself visually into a situation not immediately at hand nor, probably, within your own experience. Perhaps not easy for all to do.

Second Benchmark: Food Stamps

After just two months of instruction (the first benchmark was given in mid-October, not September) here's the second challenge Justin faced:

> You're lost in Washington, DC, find self in small room with two politicians debating whether "Congress should reverse the cuts to food stamps that happened in November (2013). One's a Democrat and one's a Republican. They're stuck in their argument, each saying the same thing over and over again. So they ask you whether Congress should restore funding, make more cuts or eliminate food stamps entirely."

Now, imagine how Justin might respond after participating in the debates between Andy and Steve on such topics as the following: Stop and Frisk; the quality of life in NYC; or restricting immigration.

Imagine they take notes on position papers/editorials supporting one side or another; draft responses, receive immediate and concrete feedback weekly and compose a final essay with Claims, Counter Claims, Evidence, Warrants and Conclusions.

After a four-sentence description of what the situation was—"the $80 billion well of food stamps has been cut by $4 billion. Should these cuts be restored?" Justin presents his case:

> Many say that the cuts should be reversed . . . Others, mainly
> Republicans argue to keep the cuts and plan to make more in
> the future. They even go as far as to say that food stamps should
> be eliminated entirely. Personally, I think food stamps should be
> saved . . .

Claim? Counter Claim? Evidence?
Then Justin continues:

> One reason food stamps should be saved is that they themselves
> have saved the lives of millions across the country. And those same
> millions are starving because the food stamp cut has taken the
> equivalent of 21 whole meals per month away from them, shows a
> study by *USA Today*. The same study reveals that the food stamp cut
> is a double loss, because the farmlands aren't being payed
> [sic] to produce the food specifically designed for food stamps
> or food in general. So not only are we losing food stamps, we're
> losing food . . .

Evidence for Claim?
He continued with a second level of evidence citing the CEO of Panera Bread who gave an interview to the newspaper *Long Island Newsday* (NY), in which he claimed that the cuts would force him, were he to try to live off food stamps, to have only $4.50 per day with which to eat.

Justin then writes:

> Opposingly, the mainly Republican-side views that food stamps are
> unnecessary and should be cut . . . Republican [Congressman, Tim
> Huelskamp, R KS] defended his position with the statement
> "I think most Americans don't think you should be getting
> something for free, especially for the able-bodied adults." So, he
> believes that we, the people, don't think struggling Americans should
> get help. But, President Obama countered with "These cuts would
> affect a broad array of Americans who are struggling to make
> ends meet."

Counter Claim and Evidence? Congressman Huelskamp's quote, used by most students in the class, came from a position paper supporting the cuts, to which all students had access as they did papers supporting restoration of said cuts.

Justin concluded this essay with this statement:

> In conclusion, the cuts to food stamps are affecting millions worldwide. In highly populated places, like New York and California, millions of children are starving because their parents don't have enough food stamps to feed them. I know their pain. I've been in their shoes. Years back, my family was struggling financially, and I went to bed hungry, starving even. I would never want anyone else to go through that.

 ## Reflective Pause

What's your analysis of Justin's critical analysis?

Andy Snyder's Analysis

Justin again provides a clear statement of his opinion. Again he names reasons. But this time further explains his reasons and also offers cited evidence to support them. Again he names a counter-claim. But this time he quotes a person who advocates the counter-claim and he also explains, in his own words, his opponent's argument. And he also uses a quote from a recognized authority to attack the central point in his opponent's counter-claim. And again Justin demonstrates the crucial capacity to re-imagine himself (in this case through actual memory) to inhabit the scenario described. Justin realizes that the scenario has real effects on real people— including people like himself.

Justin has further developed some strengths already evident in his first essay. But he's also developed some thinking practices that he significantly lacked—especially around the use of evidence, quotes, and the articulation of our ideas.

Even though "imagination" is not within the rubric, Andy has identified Justin's ability to project himself into these situations.

Why is this important, do you think?

Being able to imagine the real situation of people in different experiences may contribute to their understanding of such situations. Certainly, if Justin had not had the experience of hunger himself, he would have had quite a different judgment upon those for whom such government assistance has been cut. Consider, therefore, the importance of imagination for political action.

How to Modify Instruction after First Benchmark

A. Making the process "ritualized," as Andy described it. Follow the same pattern of instruction weekly: Focus on deepening claims and reasons; finding evidence that is accurate, representative and reliable. This helps students to internalize the thinking process.

B. Providing more opportunities and challenges for students to question the "authorities": write down their questions, share them amongst themselves and present them publicly. Require students to respond to each other's questions.

C. Using models of good critical writing. For example, most articles about scientific "discoveries" include counter claims by other scientists not yet convinced by such reports.

D. Revising drafts with peers and tutors.

E. Ensuring presence of opportunities for students to exercise personal choice amongst alternatives: topics, sources of information for arguments . . .

What will embed a new way of thinking about life situations is an ever-present series of similar questions or statements, ones that help us develop new patterns of thought. Andy Snyder and Steve Lazar were attempting to provide what some have called "thinking routines," somewhat ritualized frameworks for guiding our thinking about complex life situations.[5] My mother provided such a model of thoughtfulness when I told her that all grains of sand on a beach are unique. "How do you know?" she responded. "Have you seen them all?"

On a more formal level the school at mid-term presented all faculty with the results of students' benchmark performances. Steve Lazar, Dean of Academic Progress, laid out large butcher block posters with data related to the rubrics for each subject, ones similar to Figure 10.1 Then each teacher observed the data, analyzed it and set goals for improving students' performance during the second half of the year.

Pitfalls/Challenges

Obviously, it's in our nature to think about having reasons. But perhaps not "good reasons." Very often we'll hear kids respond with "Cuz!" "Cuz why?" "Just because!"

Not good enough.

We're used to having our own opinions and preferences—about favorite sports teams and for coffee ice cream, but we're not as used to being challenged with "Why do you think that?"

This process is far more rigorous.

It's not in our nature to even think of counter examples, for reasons that contradict our preferred ways of thinking.

This is called "Confirmation Bias," we prefer to continue thinking as we always have without challenge nor consideration of others' points of view. Years ago James Harvey Robinson wrote in *The Mind in the Making* that "most of our so-called reasoning consists in finding arguments for going on believing as we already do" (1921, p. 47). Do you agree?

Research by David Perkins of Harvard's Project Zero (1985) indicated that, in his study at least, participants from high school through college did not qualify their claims or conclusions with taking the opposite point of view:

> the typical argument in our sample concentrates on one side of the case, does not develop that side very fully, and neglects relevant counterarguments and appropriate hedges. (1985, pp. 14–16)

Too often we see and hear people in the media making claims for their preferred positions: "The way to 4% growth in our economy is to cut regulations and taxes . . ."

"One sure way to preserve the planet is to put a price on our use of carbon . . ."

Well, how do you know? What data supports each claim? What data contradicts each claim? And why do you believe either the claim or counter claim?

I doubt I've ever heard a politician present a counter claim to an argument advocating a certain position.

Purpose of Argument

Both Andy and Steve would agree that the purpose here was not "to win," as in a political contest, but to gain deeper understandings about issues.

"The goal of high school is not success," Andy told me after class. "It should be about gaining deeper understanding of an issue, being able to ask

good questions to refine or clarify it. What we need is an openness to inquiry throughout. That's how we gain wisdom."

Thus, one of our most important reasons for challenging students to think critically in all subjects is to open each one, as if it were an artichoke, to see its complexity, its layers of meaning, all related to a central core issue.

We have focused here on social studies but you can imagine the same Conclusions, Reasons, Evidence, Counter Claims arguments being drawn within language arts in analyzing character, conflict, theme and artists' intentions in *Twelfth Night*. Recall in Chapter Nine, Wilette had to gather evidence and draw conclusions about which fast food franchise to purchase. And remember Joshua's use of this framework in biological experiments.

Summarizing Philosophy

At year's end I asked Andy and other participants in this study to provide a statement of underlying philosophy that might shed light on how they teach their classes. I think Andy's is worth citing in its entirely:

> *I believe that our little private lives gain greater dignity when they intersect with a consciousness of the public good and with existential realities. So I try to involve students in a collaborative effort to "undo the folded lie" in our culture (Auden).*
>
> *In my courses we focus partly on intellectual angles—asking big questions, exploring deep contradictions, learning to discuss more powerfully (less like cartoony talking-points and more like real thinkers). But we also focus on civic participation—how to undertake successful collective action, strategizing around power and authority, building alternative systems. Part of undoing "the folded lie" involves challenging socio-political realities like wealth disparities, racism, etc. But it also involves reconsidering a way of life which has led us to lose touch with fundamental human realities like wondering, growing food, really listening to each other, and meaningfully dealing with death.*
>
> *Like many other social studies teachers I do my work because I believe in the democratic vision of public education—we help our students to become thoughtful and capable human beings who can live good lives while contributing to the renewal of our civilization.* (Personal communication, June, 2015)

We can see how important it is to ask "the big questions," ones about "deep contradictions," about conflicting forces in history and literature. One of the most interesting aspects of Andy's teaching occurred during a study of slavery when he asked each student "What questions should we be asking about slavery, about the proponents and opponents, about its history in our country?" Not a mere recitation of facts, but a deep probing for underlying assumptions, causalities and hidden connections.

Here is the "fundamental reality" of wondering, of probing with unasked questions about who we are, how we got where we are and where we want to go.

Indeed, why is there wealth inequality? A question very much worth asking by all citizens.

Andy's work splendidly exemplifies the school mission statement:

> Harvest Collegiate High School engages students in the natural process of experience, questioning, and the pursuit of precision— how people really learn. We believe in cultivating students' power to produce and reflect, rather than simply consume, as the fundamental way of being in the world.

Conclusion

So, what can we conclude after visiting Andy's classroom where students are given a weekly challenge of Take a Position, Argue it with Reasons, Evidence and Counter Claims?

Here's what some students said upon reflection. When asked, "What's the most important thing you learned last semester in Looking for an Argument?" Tony said,

> It was a lot of thinking . . . very complex compared with the ease of essay writing in my previous school (in FL) . . . He [Andy] kept extending our limits . . . [raising] our expectations . . . It was like what a lawyer had to present to a judge . . . [Valuable?] Yes.

Julia:

> It involved learning how to use evidence to support a claim and recognize when others are doing it . . . I liked it! It was fun . . . The topics were fun, like whether or not [the New York City police department policy of] Stop and Frisk was a good one . . . [With respect to arguments or claims presented in the media] A lot of times they don't do it [support claims with evidence] . . . Useable in any class where you had to organize an essay . . .

Justin:

> The class gave me the ability to consider things from the other side of the glass . . . caused me to care and understand others' point of

view . . . [Gave me] a new sense of empathy . . . Good not to take anything for granted, to understand how others felt.

Justin went on to describe how he transferred this organized way of thinking and persuading to family discussions where, when talking about the issue of food stamps (see above), he managed to raise the eyebrows of his uncle, who definitely sided with those who felt recipients needed to assume more responsibility for their lives: "Don't give something for nothing."

One surprising but welcome comment was that of Julia who acknowledged the value in recognizing when others in a discussion are supporting their positions with evidence and those in the media (commentators, politicians, experts) who are not providing evidence.

What could be more valuable for becoming a responsible citizen who keeps herself apprised of important issues, examines evidence, takes a stand but is interested in how others think and feel?

As the sign in Andy's class reminded all students: confirmation bias is searching only for evidence that supports your own point of view.

How far can democracy advance with citizens who fail to see issues from more than one point of view?

Application

1. How does Andy teach argument different from the way you do?

2. How might his approaches—modeling with a colleague, following a rather tight schedule for reaching conclusions, using his well-crafted rubric—help you and your students?

3. What is the role of student-led inquiry in your classes?

4. To what degree do students reflect on their work progress and learn from this process?

Notes

1. Jacob Bronowski was a physicist and poet who wrote elegantly about commonalities between sciences and humanities, one such was the power of our imaginations to create characters and to invent concepts—*The Identity of Man* (1971), *The Origins of Knowledge and Imagination* (1978).

2. Harvest Collegiate High School is a member of the New York Performance Standards Consortium and as such designs its own performance assessments, benchmarks and pre and post evaluations. All consortium schools are exempt from the New York State Regents exams save for ELA: www.harvestcollegiate.org/news (accessed July, 2015).

3. This study compared Fourth Graders given a week to investigate strip mining or endangered species. One group was encouraged "simply to learn facts about the material together and help one another. The other groups were presented with the same material but were encouraged to focus on unresolved controversy and their own differences of opinion surrounding the material." Those kids focusing upon "unresolved controversy . . . had learned the material much more thoroughly . . ." Why do you suppose this is so?

4. "Congressman Blank says this is a terrible policy . . . A study conducted locally finds that three out of four instances of Stop and Frisk proved to be inconsequential—no arms found . . ." What questions should students pose here?

5. See Ron Ritchart, *Intellectual Character* (2004).

References

Barell, J. (2012) *How Do We Know They're Getting Better? Assessment for 21st century minds, K–8.* Thousand Oaks, CA: Corwin Press.

Bronowski, J. (1971) *The Identity of Man.* New York: Natural History Press.

Bronowski, J. (1978) *The Origins of Knowledge and Imagination.* New Haven: Yale University Press.

C3 Standards (n.d.) *College, Career and Civic Life Framework for Social Studies State Standards: Guidance for Enhancing the Rigor of K-12 Civics, Economics, Geography, and History.* Silver Spring, MD: National Council for the Social Studies (NCSS).

Engel, S. (2011) "Children's Need to Know: Curiosity in Schools," *Harvard Educational Review,* 81(4), 625–645.

Ennis, R. (2011) "The Nature of Critical Thinking: An Outline of Critical Thinking Dispositions and Abilities." http://faculty.education.illinois.edu/rhennis/documents/TheNatureofCriticalThinking_51711_000.pdf (accessed October, 2015).

Gallavan, N.P. (2009) *Developing Performance-Based Assessments—Grades 9–12.* Thousand Oaks, CA: Corwin Press.

McPeck, J. (1981) *Critical Thinking and Education.* Oxford: Martin Robertson.

Perkins, D. (1985) "Reasoning as Imagination," *Interchange.* 16(1): 14–16.

Ritchart, R. (2004) *Intellectual Character—What it is, why it matters, and how to get it.* San Francisco: Jossey-Bass.

Robinson, J.H. (1921) *The Mind in the Making.* New York: Harper and Brothers.

Sawaya, V. (2012) "The Truth of the Matter: A Defense of Critical Thinking as the Principal Aim of Education," *Stance,* Volume 5. www.bsu.edu/libraries/virtualpress/stance/2012_spring/8Sawaya.pdf (accessed December, 2015).

Chapter 11

Reasoning about Nature

"Investigating to Answer Questions"

The same intellectual challenges are present in high school physics as we have just seen in social studies and would find in any literature class: drawing reasonable conclusions, providing good reasons with supportive evidence.

In science, however, we are seeking answers to questions or solutions to problems as befits scientific reasoning and inquiry: "How much runway does a Boeing 777 require to lift off while carrying x amount of load?" "What causes borer beetles to attack pitch pine trees in my back yard?"

The Next Generation Science Standards describe this process as: "Planning and carrying out investigations to answer questions or test solutions to problems (HS-PS 2–1)."

And New York State Science Standards describe it as: "Students will use mathematical analysis, scientific inquiry, and engineering design, as appropriate, to pose questions, seek answers, and develop solutions."

It is "developing solutions" or "testing solutions to problems" that will require our critical thinking, drawing reasonable conclusions giving good reasons and evidence.

Here, of course, we will conduct experiments that can be replicated by others, and we would anticipate that each replication would result in similar results, at least at the basic level of doing science (typical lab experiments in school).

This kind of inquiry and thinking is the essence of doing science. We do expect the same kinds of rigorous search for and use of reliable evidence.

So, yes, we are dealing with the kinds of problem solving we found in the Sandusky, OH, students' investigations about concussions and recreational facilities, but we are also dealing with the kind of critical thinking found in Andy Snyder's "Looking for an Argument" class in the previous chapter: asking good "substantive questions" and conducting investigations.

Same Data, Different Conclusions

In sciences we are often demonstrating a claim that relates one variable, speed, to others, time and distance, for example. This will result in our devising a way of thinking about these variables: $D = R \times T$.

In the case of the 777's lift off requirements and the cause of borer beetles we might draw different conclusions, especially if the verifiable data is ambiguous or may be misleading or inconclusive.

Thus, different scientists look at similar data—evidence of microbes in a Martian meteorite—and draw different conclusions. Their "healthy skepticism" might result in questions that challenge our conclusions. This kind of skeptical questioning is always part of doing and writing about science. Almost invariably, when there is an article about some major find or conclusion—"the Universe is dying out"—you will have some scientists presenting their evidence that the amount of dark energy is dwindling, but then comes the "however, some are skeptical." We should all think like scientists on some occasions.

It's just that in science we conduct experiments that should, at the introductory, basic levels, replicate similar data across each experiment.[1] And we might or might not get the same answers in science, whereas in the humanities we most often do not.

Fostering Scientific Inquiry and Critical Thinking

Here are several ways I've seen Mike foster this kind of ability to think scientifically and critically in Physics 1:

A. Using models. Place a pendulum in front of the class with these instructions: Observe, Question what you see, Generate Hypothesis, Test and Analyze results.

B. Problem solving within all of the various units of motion, force, gravity . . . in each case giving students a set of relationships to prove on their white boards, make a presentation in small groups to all classmates, present Claims, Reasons and Evidence and respond to their "What if?" questions.

C. Collaborative problem solving with B.

D. Peer teaching and tutoring.

E. Graduation-level Exhibitions with problems created by students (e.g. Boeing 777).

F. Playing with technologies, e.g. motion sensors and calculators, where we can test our hunches, conduct mini-experiments—"What if I do this?" and observe results.

G. Continual, direct and immediate feedback on problem solving, through peer and teacher critique as well as weekly quizzes and more substantive examinations.

We shall elaborate on these further, but first the benchmarks Mike uses to observe students' growth.

Several Benchmark Assessments

Let's take a look at the kinds of benchmark tests Mike gave at the beginning and end of the year. These were called PBATs for "performance-based assessment tests." Mike's school, The School of the Future, is part of a thirty-school consortium in New York that focuses upon measuring students' growth during the course of a year by administering assessments such as:

Fall: Given a water container with a launching platform for a small plastic rocket, determine the maximum height you can send such a rocket by adding milligrams of Alka-Seltzer to the water. The latter will react with the water, forming a gas that, when released, can launch the rocket.

Mid-Term: How much potassium can you add to a garden to enhance the growth of plants?

Spring: At what angles will you achieve maximum range when using a slingshot?

Appropriate New York State Standard 1: [perform] investigations that provide evidence for and test conceptual, mathematical, physical and empirical models.

All these will require students to analyze data, make calculations, interpret them and explain the reasons for their findings. In each case, students could have discovered that, with the Alka-Seltzer, for example, there was an upper limit to the milligrams of the substance you could use to lift the rocket to maximum height (200 mg).

For each experience students were to graph their findings and then do the following:

Provide a clear description of the trend.

Thoroughly discuss the meaning of this trend.

Identify whether or not the hypothesis is supported by the data.

Refer to specific points to support claims made in data analysis.

Explain the trend (different from meaning in that here he expected students to analyze relationships amongst the different variables: height, milligrams of Alka-Seltzer, pressure and volume of water).

The thinking required in these benchmark assessments involves "proportional reasoning," usually evident at the onset of adolescence (Piaget). (See Chapter Three.) It involves relationships between two or more variables, $a/b = c/d$, the ability to compare two variables to each other using multiplicative thinking. For example: "In 30 minutes, Bob reads 60 pages of a book. How long should it take him to read 150 pages?" (http://teachmath.openschoolnetwork.ca/grade-6/proportional-reasoning, accessed December, 2015)

The initial problematic situation all students confronted upon entering Physics 1 was the following:

Given a water container with a launching platform for a small plastic rocket, determine the maximum height you can send such a rocket by adding milligrams of Alka-Seltzer to the water. The latter will react with the water, forming a gas that, when released, can launch the rocket. (Figure 11.1)

Here are several students' responses. See if you can detect differences in their analytic reasoning:

Jake:

The data does support the hypothesis because when more grams of A-S were being added the height of the rocket increased. There was a point where it did decrease but then went up again to its same climax. This could of been because of some errors that were made.

Figure 11.1 Note: The overlapping circles above "ALKA SELTZER" are meant to represent the round tablets of Alka Seltzer themselves.

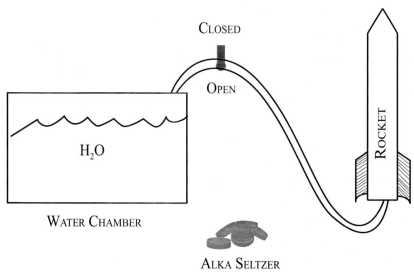

DATA ANALYSIS DIAGNOSTIC

Alice:

The graph shows that the more A-S added (g) the higher the rocket will go (ft). The conclusion is that when you increase the amount of A-S you will increase the height of the rocket. Due to the fact that the more A-S added it fuses a greater reaction. Data does support hypothesis . . . because the data shows the increase in height when there is a greater amount of A-S being added.

Diana figured it this way:

Based on the data, you can conclude that as the amount of A-S tablets added increases, the higher the rocket goes . . . However, when 200 g of A-S was added to the water chamber, the rocket's height resulted at 120 ft.

The data recorded proves the hypothesis . . . with 100 g of A-S, the rocket launched 30 ft., with 160 g, 77 ft. was reached, and at 200g of A-S 120 ft. was the new maximum height reached by the rocket.

Another student, Jonathan, added a more in-depth analysis:

This can be explained by the laws of pressure. Water can be pushed into a small amount of space to make room for other things in a sealed container, but water can only become so small, it cannot simply disappear to make more room for the new gas. Therefore, it is my theory that after 200 g of A-S, no more room is left over for gas to take up. Therefore, pressure cannot become any greater and the rocket will not travel any higher.

Reflective Pause

Even if you are not a teacher of physics, you will be able to analyze the above responses and draw some conclusions. What do you notice about these four students, about their findings and explanations? How do you explain your observations?

Who recognizes fundamental relationships within the rubric?

Figure 11.2 Science Scoring Rubric

Criterion	Examples	4 (Likert Scale)
Provides clear description of trend	Describes first part as "parabolic," second as "with zero slope"	Uses specific math vocabulary to describe "linear trend" AND describes trend completely
Thoroughly discusses meaning of trend	Explains that initially height increases as amount of A-S increases . . . but after 200 g, additional A-S has no effect	Describes relationship amongst variables completely, e.g. height + mass
Hypothesis supported?	Explains partial support	States degree to which hypothesis supported . . . accounting for complexities and anomalies
Refers to specific points to support claims in data analysis	Compares three points in first and second part	Refers to specific data points to support all claims
Supplies one possible explanation for trend seen in data after 200 g	Explains why adding more A-S has no effect	Supplies one plausible explanation using scientific concepts and logical reasoning

Moving from What to *What If?*

Mike's Analysis

Jonathan: This student not only identifies the trend in the data and discusses its meaning, but also refers to specific data points to support his claim that adding more A-S increases the max height achieved by the rocket. He reflects on the validity of the hypothesis made, saying that the data generally supports the hypothesis, but also noting that a different trend is observed in the last four tests. He tries to account for this deviation from the trend seen in the first part of the data by connecting back to science concepts from year prior, explaining that "water can only become so small, it cannot simply disappear to make more room for the new gas. Therefore, it is my theory that after 200 g of A-S, no more room is left over for gas to take up, therefore the pressure cannot become any greater, and the rocket will not travel any higher." Though the explanation is not entirely accurate (or possibly his writing lacks clarity and requires further elaboration), it's important to note that he does this without prompting. Very few other students thought to do this on their own.

Jake: This student describes the general trend seen in the first part of the data, but then goes on to identify each tiny fluctuation in the second part, rather than identifying the general trend (no change in maximum height). This student also notes that the hypothesis was generally supported except for the last few trials, but dismisses their deviation from the original trend as resulting from sources of error, which he does not identify or elaborate on. Overall, his analysis is more superficial than Jonathan's.

Diana: This student notices the basic trend that increasing the amount of A-S results in higher maximum height achieved by the rocket, and compares multiple data points to support this claim. Unfortunately, she does not address the different trend seen in the second part of her graph.

Alice: Alice's analysis may be the most basic of all the samples provided. Similar to Diana, she clearly identifies the general trend that increasing the amount of A-S increases the maximum height of the rocket. But her analysis stops there. She fails to support her claim by comparing data points and does not notice that the second part of the trend does not support the hypothesis made.

How We Modify Instruction Based upon Initial Findings

We know that some students are not, initially, good at the thinking required here. It's called "proportional reasoning" and is a characteristic of Piaget's

"Formal Operational Thought," a stage of cognitive development students enter during adolescence—or at least some do.

What we do is to provide structured tasks within supportive settings for students to begin experiencing; for example, identifying and manipulating multiple variables.

1. We teach through various models, representations of reality. The pendulum model is one of the first such exercises where students ask a lot of questions, identify the concrete variables therein as well as the abstract ones, select a question, create an hypothesis, test and evaluate results. Here we are looking to establish or validate claims about relationships amongst different pendulum elements: length of pendulum, weight, mass, height . . .

2. We identify those students like Jonathan who will become our peer leaders and tutors. On more than one occasion Mike divided up his class according to different problems students were working on and assigned a student like Jonathan to facilitate students' thinking. Sometimes students self-selected themselves to be peer tutors in small groups or in front of the entire class.

3. Another instructional approach you might use is having students keep their own inquiry/reasoning journals wherein they can not only solve a problem, but also note their thinking along the way in double-entries (Barell, 1995): problem solving on the left and reflections on the right.

4. A different proven strategy that is at work here, demonstrated to be effective by Benjamin Bloom while he was at University of Chicago, is what he called "paired problem solving" (Bloom & Broder, 1950). One person thinks aloud through the problem and the other monitors her partner's thinking, not doing any correcting, but pointing out steps that he might wish to reconsider. See Chapter Nine for how Laura used the same process successfully.

Pitfalls, Challenges

There are several challenges to fostering this kind of reasoning in sciences (and in humanities):

A. Students' levels of interest in the subject. Mike often commented upon students' differing degrees of zeal for the subject, some were far more interested than others.

B. Different cognitive levels. This kind of thinking (as mentioned in Chapter Three) requires increasing abilities to think about abstract concepts—force, motion, mass—and to be able to identify and manipulate multiple variables simultaneously. Not all students are immediately proficient in this "proportional reasoning."

C. Having to learn to think through complex, multi-variable problems that do not lend themselves to memorizing formulae. How? Asking critical questions . . . keeping notes on models of good problem-solving approaches . . .

D. The complexity of dealing with abstract concepts like "force . . . mass . . . acceleration . . . velocity . . . power . . . equilibrium." Not as easily understood as other equally abstract concepts such as "freedom . . . courage . . . love . . ." all of which have very personal, emotional meanings for most of us.

The second and third benchmark assessments were similar challenges and Mike scored each as above. At semester's end he could average data across all criteria to say that in this class students grew.

At first students were somewhat perplexed by being grading using a four-point Likert scale (Figure 11.2) and not receiving an 85% or an A.

How Does He Do It?

Teacher Enthusiasm

Having spent one day a week in Mike's Physics 1 class for an entire semester I found many characteristics present that may account for his students' progress and their genuine affection for learning physics from him. Several students wrote laudatory comments in their yearbooks: Luis noted Mike's ability to create an environment that fostered "play, exploration and curiosity." Other students noted, in their yearbook signings about "Mr. Z" as they called him: "You are always encouraging." "You have made Physics extremely fun." And another had this unexpected observation: "Your enthusiasm for what you teach is so apparent that most students thought we would get homework on graduation—ha! ha! ha!"

Obviously, teacher enthusiasm for his subject counts a great deal for students wanting to participate in physics (and noting what kind of tie he wore—for one student the "ScoobyDoo" was a favorite).

"Messing About in Science"

Playing with and exploring stuff was vital to Mike's success. When I asked him about this, he described what other observers might have called "messing about in science,"[2] that is, having time to play, explore, test out and discover key elements, for example, in a motion detector. "What does it do?" "How does it work?" "What happens if we do this?"

Depending upon how much time we allow for such structured play, we may find that our students generate all of the essential questions we had intended to ask in the first place (Hawkins, 1965).

Indeed, recent research cited in the previous chapter (Engel, 2011) confirms that under certain circumstances (with younger students), affording time to mess about, to follow one's "hunches," to experiment, make mistakes and, yes, to play around with stuff, can lead to better understanding of concepts. Again, it stands to reason that when we encourage students to "mess about," to pose their own "What if?" questions, test and examine results, that this much deeper information processing will lead to more significant comprehension and achievement.

As Engel summarizes: *"The evidence is quite clear: when children are curious, they learn. It turns out that curiosity in school is not merely a nicety but a necessity"* (2011, p. 628).

This is one way we learn, by having time, space, encouragement and peers with whom to collaborate in our playful explorations. All of science and the expansion of new knowledge could be derived from this one simple thought experiment, "What if I do this?"

Modeling in Physics

What became apparent at the beginning of the year for these students is that Mike proceeded by creating what I've called (Chapter Seven) "model experiences," ones that presented learning challenges within a framework that was duplicated time and time again.

The first model was the complex pendulum system. He set it in motion and asked students to "Describe this system."

Students thought individually, wrote notes, conferred and then shared observations:

S: I see gravity.

T: Gravity plays a role. Do you see it or infer it?

S: Infer.

T: How do you define a "pendulum"? or what a pendulum does?

S: [Gives simple description]

T: Please elaborate on this description

Mike then asked "Now, what are your questions worth investigating?"

Students worked at their tables generating ten or fifteen questions about the simple system and its multiple variables. He elicited them all and then challenged students "to identify one question you wish to answer." Then develop their hypothesis, keeping in mind the different variables they had identified.

Eventually, Mike had them work, for sake of economy of effort and maximum learning outcome from this one simple system, on a hypothesis around this question, "How does _____ affect the period of a pendulum?"

Students then conducted their own experiments, made observations, collected data and started learning how to analyze such data. For example, there would always be multiple representations—by graph, mathematical equation, written word and the model itself.

Observe, Think and Question

When confronted with the pendulum Mike introduced them to a way of analyzing it. First, Describe what you see. This requires that we become close observers of the system.

As students are observing, perhaps jotting down notes, they are, of course, thinking, reflecting on what they already know about this simple system, other systems or any of the components.

Mike concluded this phase by challenging them to pose questions of interest.

This is a very simple approach to any significant and complex system or phenomenon: Observe, Think and Question. Here is another example of a "thinking routine" we share with students so they have a framework for maneuvering through life's encounters with fascinating and complex situations.

How many of us succumb to poor initial observations?

Oh, I didn't notice that!
    If I'd only read the directions more carefully I wouldn't have put this together backwards [when attempting to assemble ready-made furniture].

The more we observe, sometimes, the more we "see" or notice.

These direct observations bring forth all sorts of remembered data, pictures, emotional sensations and interpretive frameworks. All of which might lead to our being puzzled or intrigued by what we see.

Too often people in the public eye rush to judgment before all the facts are in. I just heard a retiring four-star general of the Army (Ray Odierno) at a final press conference refraining from making any comment about a military mishap, until all the facts are in. Bravo!

And this process of observing is really far more serious and complex than merely looking at stuff. To look, examine and observe very closely requires an attentiveness just like that required to listen to one of our students when she is offering her judgment or idea. We lean closer, we take in what she is saying, process it and are ready to learn more about her thinking. The same goes for object observation: What do we see? What are the relationships inherent in the system or object or picture? How do they work? With what consequences?

It's almost as if we establish a relationship with the object. It's not just something out there. It becomes part of our conscious awareness, of our reflective presence.

Power of Students Collaborating with Each Other

Daily in Mike's classroom I see the value of students working collaboratively with each other. They solve problems at their tables, display results on white boards and offer their thinking and results to the rest of the class for critique.

As I'll note below from one of Mike's students during one of her teaching episodes, "We, students, see things differently from Mr. Z."

Why is this practice so effective?

1. Students have an audience for their ideas.

2. Having this audience means they are receiving recognition and this translates into engagement.

3. They do see the subject and its challenges differently from an adult.

4. In a small group we can get immediate feedback on our tentative ideas and questions.[3]

5. There's a long record of the efficacy of small group peer instruction.
   (Johnson, Johnson & Stanne, 2000[4])

What I see in Mike's classroom is students talking, responding, asking questions, discussing, debating, clearing up their misconceptions. When the sessions are over, we ask for large group sharing and here's where any lingering misconceptions are mediated out.

We can see students wrestling with new concepts in ways I do not remember while I was learning physics! Working collaboratively, listening to each other, building upon each other's ideas and responding to the teacher's guiding questions.

Just as important are times when students at different lab tables would serve as local experts on certain problems, and their friends would congregate around them to hear how they approached and solved a problem. Again, this expands their own repertoire of problem-solving approaches. Mike's approach isn't the only one that is given credence.

Students' Choice and Control over Material

As we noted earlier (Chapter Six), two key elements in a very engaged classroom are students having partial control of learning outcomes resulting from their having options and choices to make.

Remember Pat Burrows, an Eighth Grade language arts teacher in Catalina Foothills, AZ, who noted,

> Bottom line here . . . if my students do not feel that they have
> any power when it comes to what and how they learn, they don't
> "own" their learning and become "bystanders." (Barell, 2012,
> p. 217)

And research confirms our consideration: "When students make choices about their own learning, their engagement and achievement increases" (Davies, 2007, p. 34).

For example, students had choices over the following content areas:

1. Which questions to research (through hypotheses and experiments) with the pendulum, use of motion sensors in constant velocity problems, making quantitative predictions about objects that experience "angled forces" (resulting in the force diagrams); questions about catapults; and, ultimately, over their deeper and long-term Exhibition research studies conducted with a faculty sponsor (see P. 24, Charmain's project).

2. Designing own experiments, as in objects in free fall, testing these variables: height above surface, mass of object . . .

Making an Argument or Claim

Logical arguments may seem more appropriate in social studies, logic, philosophy or other classes (writing the persuasive essay in language arts), but here in science when we figure out the maximum amount of Alka-Seltzer by weight that can be used to launch a toy, we are, in fact, making an Argument with Claims, Reasons, Evidence and Conclusions. We are proving relationships amongst different variables just as we are in proving triangles congruent in geometry.

Teachers' Constant Probing for Deep Understanding

One of the posters hanging from the overhead in Mike's classroom describes what he calls "Probing and Pushing Questions." These include:

"What does _____ mean? How do you know?"

"Is there another way that this can be represented, explained or done?"

"What is the significance of . . .?"

"Can you predict?"

"How is this similar to or different from . . .?"

"What are some difficulties you encountered?"

"Are the models you used appropriate?"

"How would ____change if _____ is changed?"

You can hear the teacher modeling these questions constantly, and when it comes to students conducting mini teaching lessons you will hear the very same probing questions, at least from some of the students. Mike used the latter strategy more during the second year of my observations and it was thrilling to watch as students followed his model with these probing, pushing questions to enhance students' understanding.

In Andrea's teaching students who had been on a college trip for the past two days, you saw her with white board diagramming a problem of the balance of forces acting upon an object on an inclined plane. She drew what's called a Free Body Diagram as a way of figuring out the forces acting upon an object not subject to acceleration or any other unbalanced forces.[5]

Andrea:

"So, how do we start?! What would this [force] be?"

"What do we do next?"

"Does everybody agree with that?"

"Why? Why not?"

"How come we do it that way?"

"Any questions? [with good wait time, that is more than 2.3 seconds]"

"What If?" Questions

From the very beginning when Mike was working on how to graph variables and show relationships with the slope of a graph (increase in time of battery use, decreases life of battery), he was using a special kind of Pushing/Probing question:

"What if we did this?"

"What if (in battery life) we exchanged a Droid for an iPhone, what difference would that make in our slope and findings?"

These kinds of questions he especially focused upon during students' Exhibition projects, like one that tested the optimum height of release for a loop-the-loop ride at a carnival and another one where the student was investigating this question: "What is the effect of headwind on the runway length for an airplane."

Watching each of these student's independent research projects (Exhibitions) was an excellent lesson in posing these kinds of "What if?" questions to test understanding.

I watched the first young woman stand in front of two teachers and two student assessors, carefully consider the questions, usually from her teacher, Mr. Z, and often times diagram it on the board.[6]

Even without knowing the physics in depth you could tell she was wrestling with these questions that challenged her to manipulate the variables and determine a new relationship. All four assessors agreed that in both cases students had a deep grasp of the physical relationships: "When you change this ___, you see these kinds of results."

Other students, however, lacked this depth of knowledge and floundered. Their knowledge was more a set of facts without awareness and understanding of the deeper relationships between and amongst them:

If you'd understood Newton's laws better, you'd see how things
affect each other . . . You didn't see that 45 degrees is optimum. [Your]
background knowledge seemed like a collection of facts not well
integrated with understanding of relationships.

How often I heard students in this and other classes state that the reason they liked doing their projects or why they appreciated this teacher was the opportunity to see "how things fit together," meaning, I think, how concepts related to one another.

Final Benchmark Assessments

The final benchmark involved this challenge: "At what angles will you achieve maximum range when using a sling-shot?" A variation involved firing a shell.

Here's Mike's analysis of Alice's growth:

> *Alice showed the most growth of all four students. [see Application below]. On the final assessment, she not only identifies the overall trend in the data, but refers to specific data points to support her claim. She also discusses the implications of the trend, pointing out that doubling the angle of launch does not necessarily result in the range being doubled. Towards the end of her explanation, she also provides a very basic explanation for the trend ("The reason the larger angles didn't go as far because the angles were too big and the object went up instead of traveling further").*
>
> *She got better at more clearly identifying and describing the trend revealed by graphing the data. She more thoroughly addressed the hypothesis . . . There was small growth in the other areas, but she grew across all areas.*

How did he account for this growth? "She had good work habits . . . was strong in math and often came for help" (during Mike's lunch hour or after school, the invitation was always present).

How Well Did All Students Do?

Mike told me:

> *Over the course of the year, this essential skill (analyzing data) we continuously worked on honing. After the first lab experience, students individually made a preliminary analysis of their data. I then provided students with a checklist of what goes into a thorough analysis of data. I also provided them with a model, and asked them to identify each bullet on the checklist in the model analysis. Students were then given an opportunity to revise their analyses using the checklist and model as a guide. For every lab*

after that, students were given time to craft a preliminary analysis, and then their results and conclusions they white-boarded and presented to their peers in a "peer-critiquing" session. During this time, each group's results were discussed, with students often using the "probing" and "pushing" questions as a guide for thoughtful questions to ask.

"Being Cool"

These are some of the learning experiences that help students become playful explorers who are very curious about how the world works.

One yearbook endorsement stood out amongst others:

> You are awesome . . . You were a cool teacher who took work
> seriously which made me comfortable asking questions when
> I needed help and not feeling dumb.

I had not considered that taking one's subject "seriously" would foster students' inquisitiveness, but amidst the smiles, probing questions and hands-on experiments and analyzing models what came through to this student was Mike's dedication to his subject and its importance.

Conclusion

Reasoning in sciences and humanities is based upon establishing or formulating a claim and then supporting it with data or evidence. We hear in both social studies and science classes, "My claim is that . . . and here are my reasons for so stating." Then we follow with the concrete, specific data to support said claim.

What was heartening to me in both Andy's and Mike's classes was the focus upon this critical thinking process, one so vital to the life of our representative form of government. The reliance upon information, concrete, specific information, with which to make a claim or support a judgment is what civic discussions can and should be about.

So, did we really land on the surface of our one natural satellite in 1969 with Neil Armstrong stepping upon the soft lunar surface to declare, "That's one small step for a man . . . One giant leap for mankind"?

Prove it.

Figure 11.3 Alice's Final Benchmark, judging the maximum angle for launching a catapult

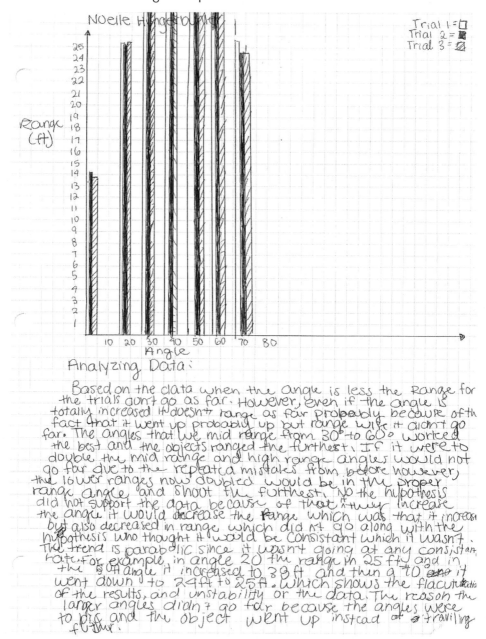

Analyzing Data:

Based on the data when the angle is less the Range for the trials don't go as far. However, even if the angle is totally increased it doesn't range as far probably because of th fact that it went up probably up but range wife it didn't go far. The angles that we mid range from 30° to 60° worked the best and the objects ranged the furthest. If it were to double the mid range and high range angles would not go far due to the repeatca mistakes from before however, the lower ranges now doubled would be in the proper range angle and shoot the furthest. No the hypothesis did not support the data because of that it they increase the angle it would decrease the range which was that it increas but also decreased in range which did nt go along with the hypothesis who thought it would be consistant which it wasn't. The trend is parabolic since it wasn't going at any consistant rate. For example, in angle 20 the range th 25 ft and in the 50 ft angle it increased to 38 ft and then a 70 ano it went down to 24ft to 25ft. Which shows the flacutatie of the results, and unstability or the data. The reason the larger angles didn't go far because the angles were to big and the object went up instead of traviling futhur.

Application

1. What is your analysis of Alice's reasoning:

   Based on the data when the angle is less . . . the range for the trials don't go as far. However, even if the angle is totally increased it doesn't range as far probably because of the fact that it went up . . . but range wise it didn't go far. The angles that we [tested at] mid range from 30 degrees to 60 degrees worked the best and the objects ranged the furthest.

   No, the hypothesis did not support the data . . . because [if you increased the angle you could decrease the range] . . . [We] *thought that it* [the relationship between angle and range] *would be constant, but it wasn't.*

   The trend is parabolic since it wasn't going at any constant rate.

   The reason the larger angles didn't go far [was because] *the angles were too big and the object went up instead of traveling further.* (see Figure 11.3)

   Clear? Cogent? Shows improvement?

2. How might you use an assessment such as this in one of your own units?

3. Wherein do you challenge students to analyze complex situations, draw conclusions—make a claim—and have to support it with good reasoning and reliable data?

4. To what extent is the reasoning included in your assessment rubrics?

Notes

1. We don't conduct the same kinds of repeatable experiments in Andy's class, but we do challenge each student with the same questions. However, we can conduct an "experiment" with the Stop and Frisk problem, by creating a hypothesis "If we cancel the program, crime will definitely rise." We might have to wait a long time to obtain results, however.

2. See the marvelous essay by David Hawkins, "Messing About in Science" (1965).

3. I credit working in collegial small groups in graduate school with helping me overcome apprehensions about asking questions in a large group—everybody knows the answer . . . too simple . . . they'll think I'm stupid . . .

4. "For Learning Together, cooperation promotes higher achievement than do competitive or individualistic efforts (effect sizes = 0.82 and 1.03 respectively)."

5. www.physicsclassroom.com/class/newtlaws/u2l2c.cfm (accessed December, 2015).

6. Her Exhibition and original research involved the length of a runway needed for maximum, effective aircraft take-off.

References

Barell, J. (1995) *Teaching for Thoughtfulness: Classroom strategies to enhance intellectual development* (2nd edn). New York: Longman.

Barell, J. (2012) *How Do We Know They're Getting Better? Assessment for 21st century minds, K–8.* Thousand Oaks, CA: Corwin Press.

Bloom, B.S., & Broder, L. (1950) *The Problem Solving Processes of College Students.* Chicago: University of Chicago Press.

Davies, A. (2007) "Involving Students in the Classroom Assessment Process." In D. Reeves (Ed.), *Ahead of the Curve: The power of assessment to transform teaching and learning.* Bloomington, IN: Solution Tree Press, pp. 31–58.

Engel, S. (2011) "Children's Need to Know: Curiosity in Schools." *Harvard Educational Review*, 81(4), 625–645.

Hawkins, D. (1965) "Messing about in Science." In: *The Informed Vision, Essays on Learning and Human Nature.* New York: Agathon Press (1974).

Johnson, D.R. Johnson, R., & Stanne, M.B. (2000) "Cooperative Learning Methods: A Meta-Analysis." Study conducted by the authors. Minneapolis: University of Minnesota.

Chapter 12

Independent Study

Martian Research

In the preceding chapters you have read how teachers in social studies, language arts, physics and math have presented to their students a variety of authentic tasks to analyze and from which to draw their own conclusions. In the case of one teacher, Tim Obergefell in Sandusky, OH, we have seen how students went out on their own into the community to find problems and figure out reasonable solutions. They were conducting original research involved in community improvement, creating their own pathways toward solutions as they met with leaders across town.

In Bozeman, MT, High School, Hannah Cebulla and Madie Kelly, a junior and senior when I first met them on Skype, engaged in a rather different kind of problem finding—locating ideal landing sites on Mars and, subsequently, figuring out where new stars were forming in the region of the constellation Cassiopeia.

Hannah and Madie, under the expert supervision of Lynn Powers, astronomy club advisor, applied for and received two slots in a competition to conduct research on Martian sites for potential landing sites and capable of sustaining life:

> Teachers from schools across the US led teams of students to conduct research on an area of Mars. Participants listened to teleconferences led by scientists in the field and then created a PowerPoint presentation for a competition in April. The winners of the competition were invited to present their findings to scientists at Arizona State University and NASA's Applied Physics Laboratory in Maryland. [Hannah and Madie] participated in MESDT during 2012/13, 2013/14 and are continuing with it in the present 2014/2015 academic year. (Lynn Powers, personal communication, September, 2014)

At first Hannah and Madie were lost in the Martian landscape. Hannah said:

> Our teacher gave us the basic rules, and just let us go. In the beginning, we had no idea where to start. We were supposed to pick a topic of research and *I remember being so used to teachers telling me every single thing I had to accomplish and everything I wasn't supposed to do or try.* This project taught me that you will never get a checklist in a scientific career. There are no answers yet, and it's up to you to figure them out. This is why I have trouble with the way students are taught in school. It's easy to get an A when you have everything you're supposed to do as a checklist, but there is no learning in that. You can't fail at something that's already done for you. (Emphasis added)

Both students were given directions, a set of analytic tools and left to fend for themselves. We will return to Hannah's theme—how real, deep and lasting learning results from our own struggle with trying to figure things out, not by following a "checklist" of what to do.

Star Formation in Cassiopeia

They did very well in the initial research competitions through MESDT (Mars Exploration Student Data Teams), because their successful presentations to NASA scientists at ASU, Brown University and Johns Hopkins University Applied Physics Laboratory allowed them to proceed to phase two with NITARP (NASA Archive Teacher Research Program): learning about and analyzing original data to determine the nature of star formation near Cassiopeia.

Hannah continues her narrative:

> Our group was taught the basics of star formation, how to gather archived data and how to analyze that data with the use of tools such as Python, DS9, and APT, that were used to conduct research on star formation in NGC 281, a young star forming region in Cassiopeia. We participated in NITARP during the 2013 calendar year . . .

Students and teachers met at Caltech to learn the basics of the analysis programs and get to know their team. Research was conducted during the summer with the use of Skype, Dropbox, Python, Excel, DS9 and APT.

NGC 281, also known as the "Pacman Nebula," results from the death of an intermediate mass star shedding its outer shell of gases. The nebula, full of dense gases and intense cosmic winds will become a stellar nursery where new stars form (see http://apod.nasa.gov/apod/ap141128.html, accessed December, 2015). Pacman is about 10,000 light years distant in Cassiopeia spanning some eighty light years in width.

Once their analyses were completed Hannah and Madie created posters to share with astrophysicists and other contestants at the annual meeting of the American Astronomical Society in Washington, DC early in 2014.

At the end of this phase of their independent research Madie concluded:

> The most important thing I discovered at the AAS meeting was how close knit and accepting the astronomical society truly is.
> I think often the sciences are made out to be highly exclusive. You must be a genius in order to make any meaningful discoveries, and there is a lot of deeply entrenched competition between scientists. But, experiencing the AAS conference has shown me that not only do people from around the country collaborate with one another to perform research, they also have a wonderful alacrity to explain their findings to everyone, no matter their intelligence level.
> (Personal communication, September, 2014)

In speaking with both young women it became readily apparent just how comfortable they were led to feel by the accomplished astronomers, most of whom held positions at prestigious universities.

Hannah noted:

> As we presented our research, I noticed the amount of respect I received from people who were clearly more experienced and more educated than I. This prompted me to pursue a career in astrophysics and possibly a degree in computer science; regardless of my grades or GPA in high school. This experience allowed me to regain confidence in my dedication, and know that I can be respected in the area which allows me to succeed.

In addition the young women told me that they were struck by how all subjects they learn in school are inter-related: "We also saw the interaction between science, math, English and communication skills, and how each of these categories is just as important as the others in the field of astrophysics."

Theirs is a reflection on the nature of authentic work in our world. It doesn't come labeled as Physics Problem 1 or History Issue 2. We use all our skills and talents to analyze what is complex in this world, addressing them from multiple points of view using skills and concepts from many disciplines in order to get to the heart of the matter.

Take "Real Live Data and Analyze It"

Lynn Powers, advisor to these two young researchers, noted that the astronomy project taught "the students how to do science, do critical thinking, and take real live data and analyze it. That's amazing."

What may be amazing is just how special an opportunity has been afforded to Hannah and Madie, to have access to as yet unanalyzed raw data:

> The Bozeman High students analyzed data from the Herschel telescope, named for the scientist who discovered invisible infrared radiation in 1800. The Herschel telescope has gathered thousands of hours of data that have been archived because NASA doesn't have enough people to analyze everything. So the space agency has invited citizen-scientists to help out. (Schontzler, 2014)

This raw data might be as fresh and unanalyzed as that found by Sabrina in her research on the problems in Sandusky, or as fresh as that found by Laura's algebra students creating viable communities in a large metropolitan area.

What We Learned Is Applicable to Others

As I spoke with these young scientists over several Skype sessions it became evident that they were acquiring invaluable lessons related to how we gain new knowledge and of the meaning of "authentic" learning.

No Learning Checklist

Again, let Hannah describe it: *"I remember being so used to teachers telling me every single thing I had to accomplish and everything I wasn't supposed to do or try.* This project taught me that you will never get a checklist in a scientific career."

Students from a young age have a knack for asking so many questions about an unfamiliar task, that the answers reduce almost to routine what they have to do. Some kids just can't handle too much ambiguity, too much messing about with trying to figure things out on their own as they did in Mike's physics class with the motion detectors.

"We're all trying to find answers," Hannah told me, "and the only way we can get to those answers is if we use the tools we've been given to try, fail, and try again."

Allowed to Fail

When Hannah first spoke about "being allowed to fail," to learn from our mistakes, I realized, as she and Madie did, how much of conventional education is a case of "failure avoidance." We must avoid being incorrect, always strive for the right answer.

But life beyond the classroom is not like that. How many of us made hundreds of errors when first learning to word process on whatever program we used. I certainly did! And it took me weeks of frustrated failures to edit a video and upload it to YouTube.

Yes, Hannah and Madie were blessed with very unusual learning experiences, ones that took them beyond classroom walls to collaborate with other students from around the country, to conduct purposeful research and to share findings with those who usually make the discoveries in this field of astronomy.

But we all can glean from their experience—what we have stressed in this volume heretofore:

Engaging in authentic learning experiences like theirs, Tim's and all the others in the book.

Making choices amongst learning pathways.

Focusing upon their own inquiry and pursuit of answers.

Learning from models—be it a pendulum, a Romantic poem, an astronomer or ourselves.

Collaborating with our peers, learning from each of them and in different ways.

Using real data with which to validate our conclusions.

Hannah and Madie make a powerful statement about learning: too often we attempt to be far too directive, providing too much teacher direction.

Let students figure out, through their own messing about, how to work equipment, how and where to find answers. Their astronomical research illustrates what learning is like on the frontiers of knowledge: complex, open, intriguing, given to many false steps from which we must learn.

What Independent Study Might Look Like

So, what would more independent study look like in our middle and high school classrooms? How would we go about developing such opportunities?

1. Within one unit per year students identify a topic of interest and conduct their own research, or collaboratively with a classmate, following criteria you and students create for posing an original question and finding answers. One high school teacher gave students this experience at the end of the year when he asked each to select a chapter from the text (not yet read) and create an original project from same. The best project, from my perspective, was a video about tornadoes created by two young men who told me they don't learn well by sitting and listening. "We like to work with our hands."

2. Afford traditional "extra credit" experiences for interested students, but again they should pose an original (for them) question, conduct meaningful research and share findings with classmates in accordance with rigorous assessment criteria.

3. Make independent study a requirement for all students as Laura does in math (Algebra 1) wherein students conduct their own studies; for example, doing statistical analyses on the relationship between ethnicity, poverty and such problems as date rape or incarceration, again in accordance with rather rigorous assessment criteria.

4. Transform your entire school into one where students must perform Exhibitions in each subject in order to graduate. Here they pose original questions under guidance of one faculty member, conduct research and present findings to a panel of faculty and students who evaluate knowledge and understanding. Of course, there are opportunities to re-submit if the first attempt does not meet benchmark criteria. Many schools follow this model.

And, yes, it might be difficult to fit any of this into a very tight schedule driven too often by preparation for State testing requirements. But schools like those who are members of the New York Performance Standards Consortium do it (and have been released from the State Regents exams except for ELA). This reflects a major commitment.

But it may come down to the question of to what degree do we wish to afford students choices within the curriculum, afford them opportunities to exercise some control over their own learning?

As Hannah said, "To try, fail, and try again." This is the essence of meaningful learning.

Conclusion

Independent study as performed by Hannah and Madie is, indeed, an advanced course in learning with experts.

But this is not to say we cannot introduce its core elements of choice, time, interest and opportunity within the regular curriculum as suggested by the two of them.

There may be a few more stars in the cosmos than there are ways of doing just this within the regular curriculum, but all it takes is imagination, commitment and working with our students to enhance their ability to dig into authentic and, yes, messy, situations to satisfy their own curiosities.

Application

1. Consider options mentioned above as ways of offering students more opportunities to conduct independent study.

2. Make experiments with different approaches if you are not currently engaged in such practices.

3. Seek advice from colleagues in your own and other schools about what makes their programs successful.

4. Examine your own assessments and learning experiences to determine the degree to which students have time and resources in order to learn from their own separate attempts, some of which will fail.

5. Provide opportunities for reflection. After experimenting with these objects, after attempting to write your own autobiography similar to that of Richard Wright or Annie Dillard, what have you learned about the process of figuring things out on your own?

6. Discuss as a class these kinds of reflections in order to modify instruction, set new goals for learning.

Reference

Schontzler, G. (2014) "Bozeman Students Present Their Research on Baby Stars," *Bozeman Daily Chronicle*, 12 January. www.bozemandailychronicle.com/news/education/bozeman-high-students-present-their-research-on-baby-stars/article_c446d5aa-7a5b-11e3-b0d4–0019bb2963f4.html (accessed August, 2015).

Chapter 13

Rude Awakening for Professional Development

The "Eye-Opener"

What do you do when a student from Germany characterizes learning in your Georgia district as doing "multiple choice tests," compared with what she's used to, that is, using what you've learned to figure out how to solve an authentic problem?

If you're Dr. Michael Duncan, Superintendent of Pike County Schools in Zebulon, GA, you listen very intently.

Here's what Magdalena Jenni, a young gymnasium—high school— student from St. Wendel, Germany, told Dr. Duncan and his team:

> I was here in Pike County as a foreign exchange student . . . In Germany we don't have any multiple choice . . . We have a lot of different classes and we have to know what we are learning. *In a test we get a scenario, and we have to use our knowledge, what we learned in class, to solve the problem* . . . Here in Pike County we had a lot of multiple choice, we don't have to study a lot, because the answer was given, we don't have to decide what was the right answer. You didn't have to understand, you're just repeating what you learned and [then] you forget it. You never really learned to solve the problem . . . [Emphasis added]

As you can tell, what Ms. Jenni is telling us presents a model of education based upon teachers' delivery of content and students demonstrating mastery of same with what I have often called "mindless memorization." I recall the precise moment before a mid-term exam in high school, one in world history, when I realized the truth of what she is saying: that I'd crammed so much stuff into my head that by the following week I would forget it. Most of it I did forget except for a few details about Garibaldi, the Red Shirts and the unification of Italy in the nineteenth century.

As you can also tell, what she has described is diametrically opposite to the rigor of academic preparation presented in each of the teaching vignettes in this book. I need only remind readers of our starting premise, from the work of Fred Newmann (1996) and John Bransford (Bransford, Brown & Cocking, 2000) that real learning results from students doing exactly what Ms. Jenni described, confronting authentic, complex problematic scenarios and then using one's knowledge to figure out how to deal with and or solve them. You shouldn't be able to "ace" a test just by cramming a whole lot of facts into your mind. Recall Hannah's comment about learning by "checklist."

Needs Assessment

So, what did Dr. Duncan and his team do with this one observation? He gathered his team to interview students at all grade levels, K–12. They asked students to describe their experiences in school. Here's a list of the statements-to-be-completed his team posed:

1. "I find my school work to be . . ."
2. "During class, I spend most of my time . . ."
3. "I wish school was . . ."
4. "In one word I'd describe my day as . . ."

From the high school, students said, "I wish school was not focused on memorization, but more on application . . . That we learned more practical stuff . . ." I find high school work to be "Overwhelming . . . busy work . . . time consuming."

From the middle school students said, "I wish school were more fun . . . more interesting . . . more centered around students."

Principals spent the day as students at all levels. From the Fourth Grade the reflections included the words "boring . . . time being wasted."

Pike County leaders concluded that what they observed:

Lacked Focus

Lacked Depth, and

Lacked Intellectual Rigor

(Pike County Strategic Plan, 2014 (personal
communications, 2015))

What an eye-opening and brave way to encounter the realities of students' lives, by asking them and by living a day in their lives.

From here, Dr. Duncan and his team filled in the continuing developments. First, they analyzed students' performance data:

> We analyzed our student achievement data in the four core areas, specifically the percentage of our students who exceed standards. We found based on similar demographic cohorts that our students underperform; that is, we should have more students exceeding on the state standardized test than we do.[1] This data, in addition to the PISA scores,[2] show we have an issue with instructional rigor and expectations.
>
> The community assisted in identifying the 4Cs along with personal responsibility and digital literacy. We conducted presentations with virtually every stakeholder group and shared with them the challenges facing our children in terms of global competition and changing role of the work force. (http://prezi.com/cpbgs5uhf1pt/?utm_campaign=share&utm_medium=copy&rc=ex0share)
>
> The principals and I facilitated discussions that led the participants to brainstorm the skills they felt were most important for our students to compete in the global economy. We simply tallied the results. We had a hunch what would evolve, but it was completely community created. We also engaged over 100 regional employers as part of creating a regional college and career charter school. The business community echoed our local stakeholders.

As with any large-scale change process Dr. Duncan and his team knew it was vital to enlist the participation of major stakeholders. Consider what this entails: having major trust that members of your community will, as you did, realize that there was a significant problem and that they had good ideas to contribute.

Vision and Goal Setting

With this kind of data, educational leaders have choices to make:

Accept it and do nothing.

Challenge reliability of data.

Accept results and decide to make changes.

Dr. Duncan and his team and, I assume, most teachers found this information unsettling and, therefore, unacceptable. So, what to do?

As with many very significant change efforts, it is best to involve the entire community in recognizing and addressing the needs.

Community Buy-In and Culture Development

Dr. Duncan described the process:

> *An initiative of this magnitude, one that involved every teacher and instructional leader was new to us. The process began with the community engagement process that identified critical thinking, creativity, communication, and collaboration as the district's instructional pillars (the 4Cs). It was quite obvious that critical thinking and the issue of rigor had to be addressed first, so we began talking with the EdLeader21 collaborative to find out how other districts around the country were building instructional capacity around critical thinking. It was important to us that the professional learning be organic and teacher-led. We desired to create a safe environment for teachers to collaboratively develop their own understanding of rigor and relevance, but, more importantly, to develop a culture whereby professionals learned how to work with one another to improve instructional delivery, teacher tasks; and, ultimately, to have student work products that demonstrated quality intellectual work.*

As Dr. Duncan notes with change of the magnitude envisioned we want all members of the community to be involved, to share in the decision-making and to, therefore, have a stake in what is about to take place.

The Rule of Thirds

It is often noted by observers of educational change like Michael Fullan (1993, 2007) that in such a large-scale district-wide change effort we will usually have a break down such as the following:

One third passionately support the change. These come out as "Champions."

One third just as strenuously oppose any modification of the status quo. "It's working. Why change it?"

The other third awaits for the change to take effect, to judge by results, to be shown how it will work.

I asked Dr. Duncan if this seemed to apply.

We started with a pilot team. They were influence leaders (some for the cause of good and some for evil :-) They evolved into champions as they recognized the quality of the process.

The next year we included roughly 1/3 of the teaching staff who were led by the previous year's anchors. We didn't hear so much about whether we should engage PD [Professional Development] around rigor because the data were so clear, but early on, we heard "our kids can't do this," which led one member of the team to respond "Then, when are you going to teach them?"

I wouldn't say everyone is won over; some are still growing in their understanding and struggling with departing from old lessons and tasks. Some teachers have decided they can't or are unwilling do this work and have opted out of the district.

Dr. Duncan noted one factor that often plays a very significant role:

The peer pressure of the group keeps the process moving forward, because the process is about reflecting on whether the instruction and tasks leads to intellectual work by the students; that is, do the instruction and tasks lead to the desired learning outcomes (input–output–impact).

Desired Outcomes

Helping structure professional development for the district was the team that focused on Authentic Intellectual Work (AIW), one that derived inspiration from the work of Fred Newmann and his associates (see Chapter One). Remember Newmann's landmark work written in 1996, *Authentic Achievement*, setting forth the principles of academic rigor involving higher levels of intellectual challenge found in everyday work conducted by adults. (See Chapters Eight and Ten on critical thinking and problem solving.)

The professional development focused upon the kinds of intellectual challenges we as teachers present to students ("teacher tasks"), whether, as Ms. Jenni noted, ones requiring only figuring out multiple choice questions or, rather, the application of learned knowledge and skills to solve authentic problems.

Dr. Duncan elaborated:

The standards include three categories (instruction, teacher tasks, and student work). We began with teacher tasks, because it felt less threatening than observing instruction. A member of the PLC [Professional Learning Community] *would volunteer to bring a task to the team to be scored against the standards. After scoring, the team would discuss ways in which the task could be strengthened and score higher in "construction of knowledge, elaborated communication, and connection to student's lives" (AIW language).*

The teacher would take the suggestions, rework the task and bring it back to be scored again. The teacher would have students complete the task, then the student work products were brought to the PLC to be scored against the standards. The question of student work would be around whether the task facilitated "analysis, disciplinary skills, and elaborated written communication" (AIW language).

"Teacher Tasks"

Here's a "teacher task" before professional development:

> Learn all the capitals of South American countries, recite them and tell where they are located.

And here's a "teacher task" (Grade Six) after professional development, requiring more focus, intellectual rigor and depth:

> Examine and analyze this photo of a typical street crossing in our community. What do you see? Formulate a list of any problems or hazards you find. Discuss your concerns with your group and develop a list of possible solutions.

Here's an obvious difference between pure memorization and recitation, and observation, analysis, problem identification and resolution. Each solution would lead to the question, "Why is your solution different from and, perhaps, better than others you rejected?"

> *Student analysis:* "Disabled people cannot get to the post to press the stoplight button."
>
> *Solutions:* "Add walk ways to the button post. We could hire a landscaper to fix the shrubs . . . Repave the walk way. Move the water hydrant. Change the rough red tiles to smooth red tiles."

Teachers would be eliciting not only problem identification and resolution but critical thinking in students' analysis of which solutions are better and why.

And, one Fourth Grade rigorous task:

Christopher Columbus and a contemporary author from *The Huffington Post*, make a claim about Columbus' treatment of Native Americans upon arrival in the Americas. Support your claim with reasons, examples, and details from both passages. Recognize and address alternate or opposing claims. (CCSS.ELA-LITERACY.W.4.1.B (www.corestandards.org/ELA-Literacy/W/4/1/b/) "Provide reasons that are supported by facts and details.")

As you will recall this is precisely the level of challenge we find in Andy Snyder's "Looking for an Argument" high school classroom. To be introduced in Grade Four to opposing claims and evidence contradicting our favored points of view is, indeed, the beginnings of high sensitivity to the accuracy of self-reports and news accounts, the commencement of our civic responsibilities.

Teacher Testimonial

Here is the shared testimony of one second grade teacher, April Teal, who was skeptical in the beginning of this very significant and all-encompassing change process. Perhaps she was of the one third that said, "Show me."

As a veteran teacher of sixteen years, I was a bit skeptical about diving into the principles of Authentic Intellectual Work. After all, how many times in my educational career had I been asked to try the "latest and greatest" new approach to teaching? However, as a teacher leader I knew I had a responsibility to study and implement the AIW model and encourage others to follow. I began my seventeenth year of teaching using the language of the AIW rubrics with my students. I used the rubrics to create meaningful learning experiences. With each new skill I introduced, I encouraged my students to understand the meaning behind why they needed to master the skill. All the while, I secretly thought, "They can't do this. It is too far above their heads."

My revelation came at the end of the fourth month of school. My students were concluding a unit of study about a few individuals who were responsible for founding the state of Georgia. The assigned task was to complete research on the individual of their choice and answer some specific questions about the historical figure. Students would share their findings with the class, and their work would be put on display at the local library. The questions I wanted my students to ponder had no right or wrong answers. They were questions such as, "How do you think this person changed history?" and "How are you like this person and how are you different?"

As my students were scattered about in small groups completing their assignment, I overheard a student, Ted, causing a commotion. I walked over to Ted thinking he was causing yet another problem in the group. As I got closer, I noticed he was vigorously tapping his pencil against his head shouting, "I know the meaning! I know the meaning!"

Intrigued, I stopped to listen. He went on to tell his group that he knew why I had taught the class about the historical figures. Before the others could ask why, he went on to tell them that I wanted the students to see that those famous people were just like him and the other students one time long ago. He shared that if they could grow up and change the world that he and his peers could do the same.

I remained where I stood, dumbfounded. I thought, "TED HAS STOLEN MY THUNDER!" After all, it was my responsibility to reveal the "big idea" and see all the lightbulbs come on. Right?

Wrong. As quickly as the thought entered my mind, it left. Suddenly, I realized something. Ted had not stolen my thunder. I had been stealing his and that of the other students in my class. Instead of allowing them to learn and make their own meaning, I was spoon-feeding MY meaning to them. I had not been giving them the chance to really discover how they learn and why. This revelation completely changed my approach to teaching, not only students but my peers as well. I stepped back and learned how to encourage my students to drive their own instruction. The results were remarkable.

Interestingly enough, Ted was not the brightest student in my class. He was not a leader and had no glaring strengths. He had transferred into my class a few weeks after school began. He had severe behavior problems and a learning disability. Ted always earned the lowest score on any assessment, and was two years behind the other students in the class. I still get excited as I wonder: if a student like Ted, who had so many cards stacked against him, learned how to think and find meaning for himself, how much more can the AIW approach offer the other students in our care?

There is so much in April's story:

1. Note the high intellectual challenge she's presented to her students: "How do you think this person changed history?" This calls for analysis evaluation of information and drawing conclusions. The second challenge calls for comparison and contrast and drawing one's own conclusions. Ted's conclusions were that he was just like his forebears, able to change history.

2. The other aspect that is of keen interest to me is what so often happens when you open the classroom to high levels of curiosity and intellectual challenge. It is often the case that students who have had different kinds of intellectual or emotional difficulties and were not, as April noted, some of the more frequent contributors, often respond surprisingly well and insightfully to higher levels of challenge.

AIW had liberated Ted to think and feel on his own, to investigate, collaborate and draw his own conclusions, not merely sit in a chair, feet flat on the floor, mind his own business and recite what the teacher expected.

The Hard Data on Students' Growth

Figure 13.1 shows the progress in Fourth Grade social studies after one year of professional development with intensive principal support. The percentage of students meeting and exceeding the state testing standard increased by 8% and the percentage of students exceeding on the state test increased by 8%. (This test, the Criterion-Referenced Competency Test was retired in 2014 and replaced with the Georgia Milestones Assessment System.)

Figure 13.1

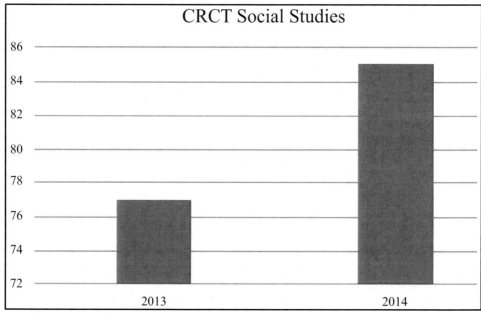

Source: Reprinted with permission.

Principal Kevin Huffstetler noted:

We had high expectations for social studies, which had been seen as underperforming for quite some time. We worked on increasing the rigor of our performance tasks, which was both scary and rewarding. What allowed us to achieve such quick, big gains was that we were all at the table together. The principal was there as a learner, not an observer. The teachers owned the products that we created, and it was a collective effort to gain consensus. (Michael Duncan, personal communication, July, 2015)

Final Thoughts from an Educational Leader and His Team

What have we learned after three years of this curricular change? The value of the change?

We learned everyone wants to improve and provide higher quality learning experiences for children, but they are not always sure what that looks like and, maybe more important, whether they can. The teams offered the non-evaluative support necessary for teachers to take risks, reflect, and grow. We had far too many fixed-mind setters, whose identity and professional worth was only as strong as the last standardized test results. A major shift in the culture is taking hold, one that values risk-taking effort, reflection, and growth. They trust the process and value input from their colleagues.

What has worked well?

The structured set aside time and the support of the leadership modeling the expectations as a learner and equal at the table.

What might we do differently in the future?

We lost a significant amount of instructional time early on as we experimented with the school calendar, but we now have a calendar that provides adequate learning time without having teachers out of the classroom.

What are we focused on now?

The focus is on linking clear expectations for rigorous instruction, teacher tasks, and student work. This will create synergy for sustainable improvement in student performance in the future.

Conclusion

This story from Pike County Schools in Georgia highlights how important educational change can successfully be initiated, implemented and managed within a large district.

The basic principles are here to be observed:

A. Identifying a real instructional need: students doing multiple choice tests rather than engaging in high-level and rigorous intellectual challenges. As we noted above, too often change is brought in for the wrong reasons: for its own sake, to respond to a marketing demand, to be like others. Good educational change is problem identification and resolution.

B. Recognizing and taking steps to meet the need.

C. Directly and persistently involving all major stakeholders—parents, teachers, students and administrators—in decision making.

D. Accessing well-proven resources to help with decision making.

E. Using leadership teams to undertake change on a limited basis with the district, allowing some to buy in and others to drop out.

F. Opportunity for participants like April Teal to experiment with a very different approach with apprehensions about being evaluated.

Dr. Duncan and his team have implemented the kinds of changes that will establish the open, trusting environment where teachers presented in this volume would thrive.

Application

1. What kinds of instructional innovations has your district undertaken? Which have worked well and why? It's important to identify what works, and why or why not.

2. To what degree does your district buy in to the major approaches of authentic intellectual work described in this chapter and throughout the book?

3. Using Dr. Duncan's approaches how might you go about diagnosing the status of your instructional program?

4. With this data how might you proceed? Possible goals and strategies?

5. Assuming some of your teachers already engage in the kinds of rigorous intellectual challenges described in this book, how might you build upon their successes? How would they become instructional leaders and sharers?

6. How would you like the story of your district's change efforts to be written? What would it say?

Notes

1. Georgia Criterion Reference Competency Test (CRCT)—all subjects. Dr. Duncan explained, "Although, I must admit these tests rarely assessed critical thinking, but based on our demographics we were underperforming." (Personal communication, June, 2015)

2. Programme for International Student Achievement. In mathematics the US ranked 27th among 34 nations tested and its scores were below average. "Students in the United States have particular weaknesses in performing mathematics tasks with higher cognitive demands, such as taking real-world situations, translating them into mathematical terms, and interpreting mathematical aspects in real-world problems." (PISA, 2012)

References

Bransford, J., Brown, A., & Cocking, R. (Eds.) (2000) *How People Learn—Brain, mind, experience, and school.* Washington, DC: National Academy Press.

Fullan, M. (1993) *Leading in a Culture of Change.* San Francisco: Jossey-Bass.

Fullan, M. (2007) *The New Meaning of Educational Change* (4th edn). New York: Teachers College Press.

Newmann, F., & Associates (1996) *Authentic Achievement: Restructuring schools for intellectual quality.* San Francisco: Jossey-Bass.

PISA (2012) "Program for International Student Achievement." Organization for Economic Cooperation and Development (OECD). www.oecd.org/pisa/key findings/PISA-2012-results-US.pdf (accessed June, 2015).

Final Words

Francesca Harrison is a recent (2015) graduate from one of the schools featured in this book, School of the Future (SOF) in New York City.

I had occasion to read all four of her final Exhibitions, those projects she undertook in each subject in order to graduate. Each was a most thoughtful, rigorous and extended analysis of an authentic and complex problem she set before herself.

I asked her to reflect on the entire experience with teachers like those featured herein, what she'd learned about becoming an educated young person ready for college. Here's what she told me.

Becoming Deep and Open Thinkers

Some of the most important things I have learned from SOF have involved depth of thinking. Not only in work and research but also in the ways we collaborate with our peers to develop our work. I have hardly looked at a textbook throughout my entire time at SOF. At first, I was highly disappointed by this. I thought it was an unfair advantage that kids at other schools would have as test takers. Perhaps that is partly true, but I have come to realize that [this school] works to develop students in a much different way.

When I talk to my peers—ranging from A students to anywhere below—no matter what their grades or test scores are—they have a certain depth of thought and understanding that I don't see in such large numbers in other places, like social media, friends from other schools, etc.

How We Learn

We learn each topic from multiple angles and point of views, we learn to form our own opinions through analysis, and most importantly, we discuss everything with our peers. Rather than having textbook opinions, we are thinkers and deep thinkers and open thinkers at that! I am so grateful to SOF for teaching me this way, because not only did it prepare me for college-level analysis and thought, but I feel prepared to go out into the world as an individual.

Exhibitions

Exhibitions themselves have also taught me a lot. At first I realized that I was learning a lot about technical skills. I developed more of an idea of time management as often times I struggled to learn how to balance my time.

Teachers were always helpful, reminding us of due dates, but of course like almost any high school student, procrastination rears its ugly head. With such a large project and such a large scope of study I realized a lot about myself as a student and writer. I learned my limits and boundaries.

For history Exhibitions I wrote about abolishing drone strikes. For English I wrote about the oppression of women through literature and in the real world. For math I wrote about how geometry could be used to deal with structural issues. For science I wrote about prevention of bacterial growth and tested out my methods of prevention.

Besides more technical lessons, I learned a lot about myself as a thinker. Coming from a busy world where social media is growing and huge world issues, events, or truths get lost, I found that Exhibitions forced me to sit down and think about the world around me, while teaching me to be a college-level writer.

Each taught me to think of one aspect of the outside world in great depth. Thus, I feel as though Exhibitions prepared me to be a good citizen in society and someone who thinks beyond the surface.

Francesca is now an undergraduate at Smith College.

Conclusion

What We Have Learned

At the end of this long journey with excellent teachers in all subjects, in secondary schools in the city and suburbs, with students of all abilities and from a wide variety of ethnic backgrounds I have some strong impressions.

Perhaps the most powerful impression stems from our German foreign exchange student, Magdalena Jenni, visiting Pike County Schools in Georgia.

Remember in the preceding chapter how she compared education at home with that in her host school system:

> In Germany we don't have any multiple choice . . . In a test we get a scenario, and we have to use our knowledge, what we learned in class, to solve the problem . . . Here in Pike County we had a lot of multiple choice, we don't have to study a lot, because the answer was given, we don't have to decide what was the right answer. You didn't have to understand, you're just repeating what you learned and [then] you forget it. You never really learned to solve the problem . . .

Notice how Magdalena lays out the requirements for good problem solving: using our knowledge, applying it to a new situation we've probably never seen before.

This is exactly what Hannah and Madie noted in doing original astrophysics research on star formation. Also, it's the same for solving any original problem like those in Sandusky (traffic accidents)—you do not have a "checklist" of steps to follow in lock step. Such a checklist is similar to an algorithm, or formula, in mathematics: $a^2 + b^2 = c^2$ (the Pythagorean theorem). Plug in the values and if you do the arithmetic accurately, you get the right answer.

In other words, doing the authentic intellectual work we've been speaking about in this book requires real thought.

It requires what British philosopher Gilbert Ryle described as the nature of thinking:

> Thinking is trying to better one's instructions; it is trying out promising tracks which will exist, if they ever do exist, only after one has stumbled exploringly over ground where they are not. (1979, p. 78)

This, of course, is precisely what Tim's and Laura's students had to do to solve problems of football concussions and to lay out an ideal community. It's what Andy's students had to do in figuring out what their stance on the federal food stamp program would be, sifting through sometimes contradictory evidence and pronouncements by politicians of different persuasions.

It's what Steve's students had to do in posing original questions about what led to the Crimean crisis.

And, of course, Mike's physics students had to figure out textbook kinds of problems related to forces, motion, acceleration, Newton's Three Laws and the like. Each might have had a correct answer, but they were allowed and encouraged to explore different approaches to these, working collaboratively with classmates and learning best ways to think about and solve them.

This is the nature of "authentic intellectual work" and of "authentic pedagogy," challenging students to engage in all of the complexities of 21st century thought: inquiry, problem solving, critical/creative and reflective thought.

Recall Francesca Harrison's eloquent and moving summation of her becoming a "deep and open thinker" in the preceding Final Words. Her reflections attest to the leadership of her teachers, her argonauts of educational change.

CCSS

In some places I've cited how the core teachers here have been using the Common Core State Standards, as well as the priorities with the C3 Social Studies standards and those in science, Next Generation Science Standards.

Whenever I asked any one of them how what they were doing related to these standards, each was able to, with a few clicks, take me right to the appropriate standards that reflected what they were doing. What this told me was that they were thoroughly familiar with which standards they were enacting at the time.

For example, Laura would, in moving from one small group to another, take two clicks on her iPad, find the relevant math CCSS and send it to me before she got to the student sprawled across his desk claiming he just hadn't figured out the problem yet. Recall, he eventually did!

This meant not only that they had studied and applied them to their work but also that they valued them as references to what should be taught within the curriculum. You can see a very practical example of just how by reflecting on Andy's and Steve's classes in argumentation and history, both which had a heavy emphasis on students' inquiry.

Change Process

Long-term change is a process, not an event, as noted many years ago by Michael Fullan (1993, 2007).

It's not easy, but Dr. Michael Duncan is not the only leader recognizing that we must move away from multiple choice and checklist toward authentic intellectual work.

We can take initial steps with any intellectual task, pre, formative and summative assessment or problematic scenario we set before our students.

Look at what we are asking our students to do and analyze it in accordance with Magdalena's criteria:

1. Can we get the correct answer by memorizing stuff and bringing it to the task?

2. Or does it require actual application of what we've learned to a novel problem?

3. By applying Hannah Cebulla's criteria: Is completing the assignment like doing a checklist, just plugging in numbers or words with no thought required?

4. Does it offer sufficient challenge so that there will necessarily be opportunities to "try, fail, and try again."

"Pick yourself up, dust yourself off and start all over again," as the Jerome Kern song lyric goes from the 1936 movie *Swing Time* with Ginger Rogers and Fred Astaire.

5. By aligning with Three Story Intellect: Do the intellectual tasks within the assignment fall within the lowest level, Gathering Information (reading the lines), or do they demand thought at Levels II and III? (See Figure 2.3.)

"We've never had problems like this!" students will say.

So, we start slowly, incrementally, with small steps on different assignments throughout the unit. We do not go all gangbusters as some states are doing with higher-level challenges in the CCSS tests and then use them to evaluate teachers. This is a wrong-headed practice.

Yes, Laura gave her students the high-level challenge to create a community project as a pre assessment, but then all during the year they were faced with similar intellectual challenges as class projects, for homework and the like—"Analyze this archeological data and figure out how far down they had to dig to get to the dinosaur bones." April Teal (Chapter Thirteen) was surprised when her second grader drew his own conclusion about the importance of leaders in Georgia! "They stole my thunder!"

No, they created their own and for some of us that is the sweetest, most rewarding sound there is, our students drawing their own well-reasoned conclusions.

What If They Don't Get It?

And what happens when students are unable to go "exploringly" over new mental operations, when they are fearful of taking the risk of being wrong, making mistakes? This is what happened to me in Algebra 1 when the teacher gave us a novel problem involving baseball. I told him, "We never studied that."

He replied, "You should have been able to analyze the problem." Not!

What then? Do we then give them a "checklist"?

No, what we need to do is what teachers here so often do, that is, model for them how to do it, how to think constructively about analyzing novel problems. What questions do we need to ask? This is what I heard a math teacher ask her students before tackling a novel problem. It is right in line with the research by Stevenson (1994), claiming that American students were less inclined to analyze than to memorize, as I did, algorithms and plug in numbers. It seems as if other teachers in Japan and China were more intent upon helping students ask good questions in order to understand and analyze a problem before grabbing hold of convenient numbers and plugging them into a formula. Often, according to Stevenson, analyzing the novel problem was the primary learning experience, not the "press for a correct answer." Here's where some will definitely go "exploringly" over search paths, make mistakes, fail, and try all over again.

We might, as Mike Zitolo so often did, provide them with encouragement from students, peers, who do get it, who can move more comfortably amidst the ambiguity of complex problem solving. Paired problem solving is one method of thinking aloud through problems pioneered by Benjamin Bloom at the University of Chicago with positive results for achievement.

We might as Laura so often did provide constant examples that challenge students to think through complex problems—analyze data from New York City's "Stop and Frisk" police program, ask questions and arrive at how to answer them. Remember, she once said, "This is a playground," experiment, have fun, we're all with you and when students did get it, she was right there to give them support and attention they required. But she allowed them at first to muck about.

If we have the means, we can do what Tim did when students out in the field recorded frustration in their notes, provide them with encouraging feedback.

One Last Thought

I mentioned in the Preface that I conceived this project after completing a similar one in 2011—*How Do We Know They're Getting Better? Assessment for 21st century minds, K–8*. I was given the go-ahead by that publisher.

But then a funny thing happened on the way to this volume, that is, three previous publishers of my work rejected the initial manuscript and multiple modifications. One prevalent reason was the difficulty of marketing to the secondary school educators. This was an amazing admission.

A very special thanks, then, to Routledge and Acquisitions Editor, Lauren Davis, for seeing the importance of what you have just read and the needs it would meet within our academic communities, both public schools and higher education. Thanks also to Lauren for her insightful re-consideration of the title: *Moving From* What *to* What If? *Teaching critical thinking with authentic inquiry and assessment*.

Thanks to her we now have a volume that speaks not only to the assessment question but equally well to the question of how we help place students in what Marzano and Toth (2014) call "the land of cognitive complexity." How do we challenge students with the kinds of experiences Gilbert Ryle describes as the essence of thinking, where we stumble "exploringly" over new territories of thought, analyzing data we've never seen, before using what we've learned about how to ask good questions, analyze and arrive at reasonable conclusions?

So, in the end this book has turned out to be as much about the heart of the matter—the learning experiences—as about the pre, formative and summative assessments we have been calling performance-based authentic assessments. Mind you, each of the aforementioned teachers has been able to convince me, and I hope you, of how their students have grown intellectually from one benchmark performance-based assessment to the next.

Each teacher within these pages is a model of excellence who sets before her or his students the highest levels of cognitive challenge.

And they thrive in the process.

So, to those loud, ill-informed politicians who claim "Our schools are failing!" let them heed the examples of these teachers and, I'm sure, teachers within their own districts who have the same high standards of rigor and cognitive complexity. Let them read Francesca's "Final Words."

One of Andy's students, after the course on Looking for an Argument, noted that she was much more alert to those shallow thinkers seeking attention who make outrageous claims without giving good reasons for them whatsoever—no reliable, relevant and significant data to support their conclusions.

To all these teachers and students I give a resounding BRAVO ZULU! Meaning "Well Done!" in terms of being argonauts and leaders of educational change, growth and development.

References

Fullan, M. (1993) *Leading in a Culture of Change*. San Francisco: Jossey-Bass.

Fullan, M. (2007) *The New Meaning of Educational Change* (4th edn). New York: Teachers College Press.

Marzano, R., & Toth, M.D. (2014) "Teaching for Rigor: A call for a critical instructional shift." West Palm Beach, FL: The Marzano Center. www.marzanocenter. com/files/Teaching-for-Rigor-20140318.pdf (accessed December, 2015).

Ryle, G. (1979) *On Thinking*. Totowa, NJ: Rowman and Littlefield.

Stevenson, H. (1994) *Learning Gap: Why our schools are failing and what we can learn from Japanese and Chinese education*. New York: Simon & Schuster.

Taylor & Francis eBooks

Helping you to choose the right eBooks for your Library

Add Routledge titles to your library's digital collection today. Taylor and Francis ebooks contains over 50,000 titles in the Humanities, Social Sciences, Behavioural Sciences, Built Environment and Law.

Choose from a range of subject packages or create your own!

Benefits for you

>> Free MARC records
>> COUNTER-compliant usage statistics
>> Flexible purchase and pricing options
>> All titles DRM-free.

Benefits for your user

>> Off-site, anytime access via Athens or referring URL
>> Print or copy pages or chapters
>> Full content search
>> Bookmark, highlight and annotate text
>> Access to thousands of pages of quality research at the click of a button.

REQUEST YOUR FREE INSTITUTIONAL TRIAL TODAY

Free Trials Available
We offer free trials to qualifying academic, corporate and government customers.

eCollections – Choose from over 30 subject eCollections, including:

Archaeology	Language Learning
Architecture	Law
Asian Studies	Literature
Business & Management	Media & Communication
Classical Studies	Middle East Studies
Construction	Music
Creative & Media Arts	Philosophy
Criminology & Criminal Justice	Planning
Economics	Politics
Education	Psychology & Mental Health
Energy	Religion
Engineering	Security
English Language & Linguistics	Social Work
Environment & Sustainability	Sociology
Geography	Sport
Health Studies	Theatre & Performance
History	Tourism, Hospitality & Events

For more information, pricing enquiries or to order a free trial, please contact your local sales team:
www.tandfebooks.com/page/sales

 Routledge
Taylor & Francis Group

The home of
Routledge books

www.tandfebooks.com